D1305700

LILIAN S. BESORE
MEMORIAL LIBRARY

FRANKLIN COUNTY LIBRARY SYSTEM
101 RAGGED EDGE ROAD SOUTH
CHAMBERSBURG, PA 17202

BESORE MEMORIAL LIBRARY
305 E. BALTIMORE ST.
GREENCASTLE, PA 17225

THIS BOOK BELONGS TO:

_____

_____

_____

_____

LET FREEDOM RING!

p

This is a Parragon Publishing Book
This edition published in 2006

Parragon Publishing
Queen Street House
4 Queen Street
Bath BA1 1HE, UK

Project Director: Natasha Tabori Fried
Designer: Jon Glick
Recipes: Lena Tabori
Facts: Rachel Hertz
Additional fact-checking & copyediting: Jana Martin
Editorial Assistants: Lawrence Chesler, Deidra Garcia

Copyright © 2006 Welcome Enterprises, Inc.

All rights reserved. No part of this book may be reproduced or utilized in any form or by any means, electronic or mechanical, including photocopying, recording, or by any information storage or retrieval system, without permission in writing from the copyright holders.

Printed in Singapore

10 9 8 7 6 5 4 3 2 1

CONTENTS

THE WHOLE WORLD IS COMING

LAKOTA GHOST DANCE SONG, CIRCA 1880

The whole world is coming.
A nation is coming, a nation is coming,
The Eagle has brought the message to the tribe.
The father says so, the father says so.
Over the whole earth they are coming.
The buffalo are coming, the buffalo are coming,
The crow has brought the message to the tribe,
The father says so, the father says so.

POWHATAN TO CAPTAIN JOHN SMITH

JAMESTOWN, VIRGINIA, 1609

Despite the life-saving aid that Powhatan Confederacy tribes gave the first English settlers in Jamestown, the settlers abused the friendship. Conflicts arose over land and the trading of weapons and food. Powhatan (Chief Wahunsonacock), chief of the Powhatan Confederacy and the father of Pocahontas, addressed Captain John Smith with this warning.

I AM NOW GROWN OLD, and must soon die; and the succession must descend, in order, to my brothers, Opitchapan, Opekankanough, and Catataugh, and then to my two sisters, and their two daughters. I wish their experience was equal to mine; and that your love to us might not be less than ours to you.

Why should you take by force that from us which you can have by love? Why should you destroy us, who have provided you with food? What can you get by war? We can hide our provisions, and fly into the woods; and then you must consequently famish by wronging your friends. What is the cause of your jealousy? You see us unarmed, and willing to supply your wants, if you will come in a friendly manner, and not with swords and guns, as to invade an enemy.

I am not so simple, as not to know it is better to eat good meat, lie well, and sleep quietly with my women and children; to laugh and be merry with the English; and, being their friend, to have copper, hatchets, and whatever else I want, than to fly from all, to lie cold in the woods, feed upon acorns, roots, and such trash, and to be so hunted, that I cannot rest, eat, or sleep. In such circumstances, my men must watch, and if a twig should but break, all would cry out, "Here comes Captain Smith"; and so, in this miserable manner, to end my miserable life; and, Captain Smith, this might be soon your fate too, through your rashness and unadvisedness.

I, therefore, exhort you to peaceable councils; and, above all, I insist that the guns and swords, the cause of all our jealousy and uneasiness, be removed and sent away.

The Wild West

On October 26, 1881, the Earp brothers (Wyatt, Virgil, and Morgan) and Doc Holliday faced down the Clanton Gang in a 30-second hail of bullets behind the OK Corral in Tombstone, Arizona. When it was over, Virgil and Morgan were wounded and three outlaws lay dead.

Doc Holliday (1851–1887) was a dentist by trade who moved West for his health.

Wyatt Earp (1848–1929) was a gambler and a law man who roamed the West from Illinois to Alaska.

Born Martha Jane Cannary in Princeton, Missouri, Calamity Jane (1852–1903) was orphaned as a young girl. She made her way working anywhere from mining camps to dance halls. A drinker, talker and smoker who shot like a man, she claimed to have married Wild Bill Hickok.

There was truth to the legends surrounding Wild Bill Hickok (1837–1876): a farmhand, stagecoach driver and hired gun, he worked as a Union army spy and served as a Marshall on the rough frontier after the Civil War.

Crazy Horse (1844–1877), chief of the Oglala Sioux, refused to be pushed onto a reservation. He united Sioux and Cheyenne forces to defeat General Custer and his troops at Little Bighorn, but ultimately surrendered in order to survive.

Geronimo (1829–1909), though not a chief, was recognized as a leader of the Chiricahua Apache. After being forced onto a barren reservation in Arizona, he led a number of revolts. Years of conflict ended in Geronimo's surrender, and he died in detention.

General George Armstrong Custer (1839–1876) earned his reputation in the campaigns against the Indians in South Dakota and Montana, as well as in the Civil War. He was killed at Little Bighorn, where his men were defeated by Lakota, Cheyenne and Arapaho warriors.

Teton Sioux Chief Sitting Bull (1831–1890) was instrumental in annihilating General Custer's attacking forces, but lived on to see his people surrender and move to reservations. Late in his life, he traveled with Buffalo Bill's Wild West show.

"Buffalo" Bill Cody (1846–1917) was a champion buffalo hunter, army scout and founder of Buffalo Bill's Wild West, a traveling show that began the rodeo and toured America and Europe.

ALEXANDRA DREW HER SHAWL CLOSER about her and stood leaning against the frame of the mill, looking at the stars which glittered so keenly through the frosty autumn air. She always loved to watch them, to think of their vastness and distance, and of their ordered march. It fortified her to reflect upon the great operations of nature, and when she thought of the law that lay behind them, she felt a sense of personal security. That night she had a new consciousness of the country, felt almost a new relation to it. Even her talk with the boys had not taken away the feeling that had overwhelmed her when she drove back to the Divide that afternoon. She had never known before how much the country meant to her. The chirping of the insects down in the long grass had been like the sweetest music. She had felt as if her heart were hiding down there, somewhere, with the quail and the plover and all the little wild things that crooned or buzzed in the sun. Under the long shaggy ridges, she felt the future stirring.

BARBECUED RIBS

American barbecue was first popularized on the cattle drives of the late 1800s, when cowboys slow-roasted tough meat to make it more palatable. The barbecue sauce was created using a New World staple: tomatoes.

3 cups ketchup

1 cup chili sauce

grated zest of 1 lemon

Juice of 2 large lemon

$1/4$ cup French's mustard

1 $1/2$ tablespoons Tabasco sauce

$1/4$ cup Worcestershire sauce

2 tablespoons molasses

2 tablespoons brown sugar

2 cloves garlic, chopped

$1/4$ cup chopped parsley

2 tablespoons apple cider vinegar

salt and pepper to taste

3 pounds beef ribs

1. In a large heavy skillet, combine all of the ingredients (except the ribs) and warm through over low heat. Do not bring to a boil.

2. Remove, cool and use half the mixture to rub all sides of the meat 1 hour before grilling.

3. Prepare the grill and ignite the charcoal.

4. Grill the ribs over medium–hot coals until tender (1 hour or so). Keep basting and make sure you turn them frequently so they don't burn.

5. Continue cooking for 20–25 minutes until done. (You can also do these in the oven: preheat oven to 325° F and place the ribs in a shallow baking pan. Cover with half the sauce. Bake in the center of the oven for 1–1 $1/2$ hour depending on the size. Turn and baste frequently with the remaining sauce.)

Serves 6 to 8.

Potato Salad

¹/₃ cup chicken stock

2 tablespoons cider vinegar

2 pounds large potatoes, peeled, cooked and sliced

1 cup mayonnaise

2 tablespoons Dijon mustard

²/₃ cup finely chopped scallions

¹/₂ cup finely chopped celery

3 tablespoons or so finely chopped fresh chives

salt and pepper to taste

1. Mix the chicken stock and the vinegar and pour over the potatoes.

2. In a separate bowl, mix the mayonnaise and Dijon mustard. Add the scallions, celery and chives. Combine with the potatoes, mixing gently.

3. Season to taste with salt and pepper.

4. Cover and refrigerate for at least an hour. Let stand at room temperature for 20 minutes before serving.

5. Serve with barbecued ribs and slices of fresh watermelon.

Serves 4 to 6.

BATTLE HYMN OF THE REPUBLIC

JULIA WARD HOWE, 1862

Mine eyes have seen the glory of the coming of the Lord:
He is trampling out the vintage where the grapes of wrath are stored;
He hath loosed the fateful lightning of his terrible swift sword:
   His truth is marching on.

   Chorus
   Glory, glory hallelujah,
   Glory, glory hallelujah,
   Glory, glory hallelujah,
   His truth is marching on.

I have seen Him in the watch-fires of a hundred circling camps;
They have builded Him an altar in the evening dews and damps;
I can read His righteous sentence by the dim and flaring lamps.
   His day is marching on.

I have read a fiery gospel, writ in burnished rows of steel:
"As ye deal with my contemners, so with you my grace shall deal;
Let the Hero, born of woman, crush the serpent with his heel,
   Since God is marching on."

He has sounded forth the trumpet that shall never call retreat;
He is sifting out the hearts of men before His judgment-seat:
Oh! be swift, my soul, to answer Him! be jubilant, my feet!
    Our God is marching on.

In the beauty of the lilies Christ was born across the sea,
With a glory in his bosom that transfigures you and me:
As he died to make men holy, let us die to make men free,
    While God is marching on.

WILLIAM COBBETT
TO MISS RACHEL SMITHERS
PHILADELPHIA, JULY 6, 1794

Like many English, William Cobbett arrived in America in 1792 with high hopes. In an excerpt from his letter to friend Rachel Smithers back in England, he expressed his disappointment.

This country is good for getting money, that is to say, if a person is industrious and enterprising. In every other respect the country is miserable. Exactly the contrary of what I expected. The land is bad, rocky; houses wretched; roads impassable after the least rain. Fruit in quantity, but good for nothing. One apple or peach in England or France is worth a bushel of them here. The seasons are detestable. All is burning or freezing. There is no spring or autumn. The weather is so very inconstant that you are never sure for an hour, a single hour at a time. Last night we made a fire to sit by, and to-day it is scorching hot. The whole month of March was so hot that we could hardly bear our clothes, and three parts of the month of June there was frost every night, and so cold in the day-time that we were obliged to wear great-coats. The people are worthy of the country—cheating, sly, roguish gang. Strangers make fortunes here in spite of all this, particularly the English. The natives are by nature idle, and seek to live by cheating, while foreigners, being industrious, seek no other means than those dictated by integrity, and are sure to meet with encouragement even from the idle and roguish themselves; for, however roguish a man may be, he always loves to deal with an honest man. You have perhaps heard of the plague being at Philadelphia last year. It was no plague; it was a fever of the country, and is by no means extra-ordinary among the Americans. In the fall of the year almost every person, in every place, has a spell of fever that is called fall-fever. It is often fatal, and the only way to avoid it is to quit the country. But this fever is not all. Every month has its particular malady. In July, for example, everybody almost, or at least one half of the people, are taken with vomitings for several days at a time; they often carry off the patient, and almost always children. In short, the country is altogether detestable....

Wm. Cobbett

The American Revolution

The Boston Tea Party—a protest against British taxes and Britain's monopoly on the tea trade on December 16th of 1773—involved colonists boarding British ships dressed as Mohawk Indians and dumping 342 crates of tea into Boston Harbor. What sort of tea? Darjeeling.

A leader in the American Revolution, Samuel Adams (1722–1803) was a founder of the Sons of Liberty, organized the Boston Tea Party and signed the Declaration of Independence.

As an express rider for the Massachusetts Committee of Safety, silversmith Paul Revere (1734–1818) took two heroic rides. During the first—in December 1774— he warned New Hampshire of a potential British landing.

Immortalized in verse by Longfellow, Revere's more famous ride took place April 18, 1775, when he raced to Lexington to warn that the British were headed for Concord. He was caught, but fellow rider William Dawes made it through. When the British arrived, the Minutemen were there to meet them. The shots fired began the war.

Patriot, lawyer and Virginia governor Patrick Henry (1736–1799) uttered the words "Give me liberty or give me death," and was largely responsible for correcting the new Constitution's shortcomings with the Bill of Rights.

Thomas Jefferson's first draft of the Declaration of Independence included a passage blaming George III for the slave trade. Congress struck it out.

Founding father Alexander Hamilton (1757–1804), the country's first treasury secretary, was killed in a duel with political opponent Aaron Burr.

Seamstress Betsy Ross (1752–1836) was asked by George Washington to sew the first American flag in May, 1776. The original little resembles the current flag, but the stars and stripes were present from the beginning.

It's said that John Hancock (1737–1793) made his signature on the Declaration of Independence big enough for the British king to read without putting on his glasses.

After the war, Noah Webster (1758–1843) created the first genuinely American Dictionary: *A Compendious Dictionary of the English Language* (1806).

Though we celebrate on July 4th, the colonies actually voted for independence July 2, 1776, and the Declaration of Independence wasn't signed by all members of Congress until August 2.

The war ended October 19, 1781, in Yorktown, Virginia. There, Lord Cornwallis surrendered to George Washington and French General Comte de Rochambeau.

GIVE ME LIBERTY OR GIVE ME DEATH

PATRICK HENRY, RICHMOND, VIRGINIA, MARCH 23, 1775

*Patrick Henry, a self-taught lawyer, stood up before a meeting
of 122 delegates and virtually galvanized the room into revolution.*

MR. PRESIDENT, it is natural to man to indulge in the illusions of hope. We are apt to shut our eyes against a painful truth, and listen to the song of that siren till she transforms us into beasts. Is this the part of wise men, engaged in a great and arduous struggle for liberty? Are we disposed to be of the number of those who, having eyes, see not, and, having ears, hear not, the things which so nearly concern their temporal salvation? For my part, whatever anguish of spirit it may cost, I am willing to know the whole truth, to know the worst, and to provide for it....

Sir, we have done everything that could be done, to avert the storm which is now coming on. We have petitioned, we have remonstrated, we have supplicated, we have prostrated ourselves before the throne, and have implored its interposition to arrest the tyrannical hands of the ministry and parliament. Our petitions have been slighted, our remonstrances have produced additional violence and insult, our supplications have been disregarded, and we have been spurned with contempt from the foot of the throne! In vain, after these things, may we indulge the fond hope of peace and reconciliation. There is no longer any room for hope. If we wish to be free, if we mean to preserve inviolate those inestimable privileges for which we have been so long contending, if we mean not basely to abandon the noble struggle in which we have been so long engaged, and which we have pledged ourselves never to abandon until the glorious object of our contest shall be obtained, we must fight! I repeat it, sir, we must fight! An appeal to arms and to the God of Hosts is all that is left us.

They tell us, sir, that we are weak, unable to cope with so formidable an adversary. But when shall we be stronger? Will it be the next week or the next year? Will it be when we are totally disarmed, and when a British guard shall be stationed in every house? Shall we gather strength by irresolution and inaction? Shall we acquire the means of effectual resistance, by lying supinely on our backs, and hugging the delusive phantom of hope until our enemies shall have bound us hand and foot? Sir, we are not weak, if we make proper use of those means which the God of nature hath placed in our power. Three millions of people, armed in the holy cause of liberty, and in such a country as that which we possess, are invincible by any force which our enemy can send against us. Besides, sir, we shall not fight our battles alone. There is a just God who presides over the destinies of nations, and who will raise up friends to fight our battles for us. The battle, sir, is not to the strong alone; it is to the vigilant, the active, the brave. Besides, sir, we have no election. If we were base enough to desire it, it is now too late to retire from the contest. There is no retreat but in submission and slavery! Our chains are forged! Their clanking may be heard on the plains of Boston! The war is inevitable—and let it come! I repeat, sir, let it come!

It is in vain, sir, to extenuate the matter. Gentlemen may cry, Peace, Peace, but there is no peace. The next gale that sweeps from the north will bring to our ears the clash of resounding arms! Our brethren are already in the field! Why stand we here idle? What is it that gentlemen wish? What would they have? Is life so dear, or peace so sweet, as to be purchased at the price of chains and slavery? Forbid it, Almighty God! I know not what course others may take, but as for me, give me liberty or give me death!

George Washington to Martha Washington

Philadelphia, June 18, 1775

When the American Rebels decided to take on the crown for independence, they nominated George Washington to be "Commander of All Continental Forces," at the Second Continental Congress in the summer of 1775. He accepted the challenge to turn the ragged and inexperienced group of men into a fighting force, but refused any pay. Three days later, Washington wrote to his wife, Martha, about his appointment.

My Dearest:

I am now set down to write to you on a subject which fills me with inexpressible concern, and this concern is greatly aggravated and increased, when I reflect upon the uneasiness I know it will give you. It has been determined in Congress, that the whole army raised for the defense of the American cause shall be put under my care, and that it is necessary for me to proceed immediately to Boston to take upon me the command of it.

You may believe me, my dear Patsy, when I assure you, in the most solemn manner that, so far from seeking this appointment, I have used every endeavor in my power to avoid it, not only from my unwillingness to part with you and the family, but from consciousness of its being a trust too great for my capacity, and that I should enjoy more real happiness in one month with you at home, than I have the most distant prospect of finding abroad, if my stay were to be seven times seven years. But as it has been a kind of destiny, that has thrown me upon this service, I shall hope that my undertaking is designed to answer some good purpose. You might, and I suppose did perceive, from the tenor of my letters, that I was apprehensive I could not avoid this appointment, as I did not pretend to intimate when I should return. That was the case. It was utterly out of my power to refuse this appointment, without exposing my character to such censures, as would have reflected dishonor upon myself, and given pain to my friends. This, I am sure, could not, and ought not, to be pleasing to you, and must have lessened me considerably in my own esteem. I shall rely, therefore, confidently on that Providence, which has heretofore preserved and been bountiful to me, not doubting but that I shall return safe to you in the fall. I shall feel no pain from the toil or the danger of the campaign; my unhappiness will flow from the uneasiness I know you will feel from being left alone. I therefore beg, that you will summon your whole fortitude, and pass your time as agreeably as possible....

As life is always uncertain, and common prudence dictates to every man the necessity of settling his temporal concerns, while it is in his power, and while the mind is calm and undisturbed, I have, since I came to this place (for I had not the time to do it before I left home) got Colonel Pendleton to draft a will for me, by the directions I gave him, which will I now enclose. The provision made for you in case of my death will, I hope, be agreeable.

I shall add nothing more, as I have several letters to write, but to desire that you will remember me to your friends, and to assure you that I am with the most unfeigned regard, my dear Patsy, your affectionate, &c.

G. Washington

Presidents

George Washington (no party affiliation), served 1789–1797

John Adams (Federalist), served 1797–1801

Thomas Jefferson (Democratic-Republican), served 1801–1809

James Madison (D-R), served 1809–1817

James Monroe (D-R), served 1817–1825

John Quincy Adams (D-R), served 1825–1829

Andrew Jackson (D), served 1829–1837

Martin Van Buren (D), served 1837–1841

William Henry Harrison (Whig), served March 1841–April 4, 1841 (died of pneumonia in office)

John Tyler (Whig), served 1841–1845.

James Knox Polk (D), served 1845–1849

Zachary Taylor (Whig), served March 1849–July 9, 1850 (died of illness in office)

Millard Fillmore (Whig), served 1850–1853

Franklin Pierce (D), served 1853–1857

James Buchanan (D), served 1857–1861

Abraham Lincoln (R), served March 1861–April 15, 1865 (assassinated in office)

Andrew Johnson (National Union), served 1865–1869

Ulysses S. Grant (R), served 1869–1877

Rutherford B. Hayes (R), served 1877–1881

James A. Garfield (R), served March 1881–September 17, 1881 (assassinated in office)

Chester A. Arthur (R), served 1881–1885

Grover Cleveland (D), served 1885–1889

Benjamin Harrison (R), served 1889–1893

Grover Cleveland (D), served 1893–1897

William Mckinley (R), served March 1897–September 14, 1901 (assassinated in office)

Theodore Roosevelt (R), served 1901–1909

William H. Taft (R), served 1909–1913

Woodrow Wilson (D), served 1913–1921

Warren G. Harding (R), served March 1921–August 2, 1923 (died of a heart attack in office)

Calvin Coolidge (R), served 1923–1929

Herbert C. Hoover (R), served 1929–1933

Franklin D. Roosevelt (D), served March 1933–April 12, 1945 (died of a cerebral hemorrhage in office)

Harry S. Truman (D), served 1945–1953

Dwight David Eisenhower (R), served 1953–1961

John F. Kennedy (D), served January 1961–November 22, 1963 (assassinated in office)

Lyndon B. Johnson (D), served 1963–1969

Richard M. Nixon (R), served January 1969–August 9, 1974 (resigned)

Gerald R. Ford (R), served 1974–1977

James E. Carter (D), served 1977–1981

Ronald W. Reagan (R), served 1981–1989

George H.W. Bush (R), served 1989–1993

William J. Clinton (D), served 1993–2001

George W. Bush (R), served 2001–Present

Seven presidents served one-year terms under the Articles of Confederation before George Washington was the first president elected under the new Constitution. The seven: John Hanson (1781–1782), Elias Boudinot (1782–1783), Thomas Mifflin (1783–1784), Richard Henry Lee (1784–1785), Nathan Gorman (1785–1786), Arthur St. Clair (1786–1787), and Cyrus Griffin (1787–1788).

John Adams and his friend Thomas Jefferson died on the same day—July 4, 1826. Adams died first. His last words were, "Thomas Jefferson still survives."

Thomas Jefferson liked to answer the White House door himself—often in slippers.

James Buchanan was the only bachelor president.

Grover Cleveland was the only president to serve two non-consecutive terms.

In 1906, Teddy Roosevelt was the first president to receive a Nobel Peace Prize, for mediating a peace agreement between Russia and Japan. Woodrow Wilson was the second: he won in 1919 for creating the League of Nations.

At 6'4" and over 300 lbs, William Howard Taft was our biggest president.

Sheep grazed on Woodrow Wilson's White House lawn during WW I. Their wool was sold to profit the Red Cross.

FDR was the only president elected to three terms.

JFK was America's first Catholic president.

Gerald Ford and his wife, Betty, worked as models before they married.

Jimmy Carter was the first American president born in a hospital.

PAUL REVERE'S RIDE

Henry Wadsworth Longfellow, 1860 (set in 1775)

Listen, my children, and you shall hear
Of the midnight ride of Paul Revere,
On the eighteenth of April, in Seventy-five;
Hardly a man is now alive
Who remembers that famous day and year.

He said to his friend, "If the British march
By land or sea from the town to-night,
Hang a lantern aloft in the belfry arch
Of the North Church tower as a signal light,—
One, if by land, and two, if by sea;
And I on the opposite shore will be,
Ready to ride and spread the alarm
Through every Middlesex village and farm,
For the country folk to be up and to arm."

Then he said, "Good night!" and with muffled oar
Silently rowed to the Charlestown shore,
Just as the moon rose over the bay,
Where swinging wide at her moorings lay
The Somerset, British man-of-war;

A PHANTOM SHIP, WITH EACH MAST AND SPAR

ACROSS THE MOON LIKE A PRISON BAR,

AND A HUGE BLACK HULK, THAT WAS MAGNIFIED

BY ITS OWN REFLECTION IN THE TIDE.

MEANWHILE, HIS FRIEND, THROUGH ALLEY AND STREET,

WANDERS AND WATCHES WITH EAGER EARS,

TILL IN THE SILENCE AROUND HIM HE HEARS

THE MUSTER OF MEN AT THE BARRACK DOOR,

THE SOUND OF ARMS, AND THE TRAMP OF FEET,

AND THE MEASURED TREAD OF THE GRENADIERS,

MARCHING DOWN TO THEIR BOATS ON THE SHORE.

THEN HE CLIMBED THE TOWER OF THE OLD NORTH CHURCH,

BY THE WOODEN STAIRS, WITH STEALTHY TREAD,

TO THE BELFRY-CHAMBER OVERHEAD,

AND STARTLED THE PIGEONS FROM THEIR PERCH

ON THE SOMBRE RAFTERS, THAT ROUND HIM MADE

MASSES AND MOVING SHAPES OF SHADE,—

BY THE TREMBLING LADDER, STEEP AND TALL,

TO THE HIGHEST WINDOW IN THE WALL,

WHERE HE PAUSED TO LISTEN AND LOOK DOWN

A MOMENT ON THE ROOFS OF THE TOWN,

AND THE MOONLIGHT FLOWING OVER ALL....

A MOMENT ONLY HE FEELS THE SPELL
OF THE PLACE AND THE HOUR, AND THE SECRET DREAD
OF THE LONELY BELFRY AND THE DEAD;
FOR SUDDENLY ALL HIS THOUGHTS ARE BENT
ON A SHADOWY SOMETHING FAR AWAY,
WHERE THE RIVER WIDENS TO MEET THE BAY,—
A LINE OF BLACK THAT BENDS AND FLOATS
ON THE RISING TIDE, LIKE A BRIDGE OF BOATS.

MEANWHILE, IMPATIENT TO MOUNT AND RIDE,
BOOTED AND SPURRED, WITH A HEAVY STRIDE
ON THE OPPOSITE SHORE WALKED PAUL REVERE.
NOW HE PATTED HIS HORSE'S SIDE,
NOW GAZED AT THE LANDSCAPE FAR AND NEAR,
THEN, IMPETUOUS, STAMPED THE EARTH,
AND TURNED AND TIGHTENED HIS SADDLE-GIRTH;
BUT MOSTLY HE WATCHED WITH EAGER SEARCH
THE BELFRY-TOWER OF THE OLD NORTH CHURCH,
AS IT ROSE ABOVE THE GRAVES ON THE HILL,
LONELY AND SPECTRAL AND SOMBRE AND STILL.
AND LO! AS HE LOOKS, ON THE BELFRY'S HEIGHT
A GLIMMER, AND THEN A GLEAM OF LIGHT!

* * *

You know the rest. In the books you have read,
How the British Regulars fired and fled,—
How the farmers gave them ball for ball,
From behind each fence and farm-yard wall,
Chasing the red-coats down the lane,
Then crossing the fields to emerge again
Under the trees at the turn of the road,
And only pausing to fire and load.

So through the night rode Paul Revere;
And so through the night went his cry of alarm
To every Middlesex village and farm,—
A cry of defiance and not of fear,
A voice in the darkness, a knock at the door,
And a word that shall echo forevermore!
For, borne on the night-wind of the Past,
Through all our history, to the last,
In the hour of darkness and peril and need,
The people will waken and listen to hear
The hurrying hoof-beats of that steed,
And the midnight message of Paul Revere.

Thomas Jefferson to James Madison

Paris, December 20, 1787

Thomas Jefferson was in Paris during the Continental Congress, but received a draft of the document and report of the goings-on from friend James Madison. Jefferson's response, excerpted here, includes a persuasive argument for a bill of rights.

I like much the general idea of framing a government, which should go on of itself, peaceably, without needing continual recurrence to the State legislatures. I like the organization of the government into legislative, judiciary and executive. I like the power given the legislature to levy taxes, and for that reason solely, I approve of the greater House being chosen by the people directly....I am captivated by the compromise of the opposite claims of the great and little States, of the latter to equal, and the former to proportional influence. I am much pleased too, with the substitution of the method of voting by person, instead of that of voting by States; and I like the negative given to the Executive, conjointly with a third of either House....

I will now tell you what I do not like. First, the omission of a bill of rights, providing clearly, and without the aid of sophism, for freedom of religion, freedom of the press, protection against standing armies, restriction of monopolies, the eternal and unremitting force of the habeas corpus laws, and trials by jury in all matters of fact triable by the laws of the land, and not by the laws of nations. . . . I have a right to nothing, which another has a right to take away; and Congress will have a right to take away trials by jury in all civil cases. Let me add, that a bill of rights is what the people are entitled to against every government on earth, general or particular, and what no just government should refuse, or rest on inference. . . .

At all events, I hope you will not be discouraged from making other trials, if the present one should fail. We are never permitted to despair of the commonwealth. I have thus told you freely what I like, and what I dislike, merely as a matter of curiosity; for I know it is not in my power to offer matter of information to your judgment, which has been formed after hearing and weighing everything which the wisdom of man could offer on these subjects. I own, I am not a friend to a very energetic government. It is always oppressive. It places the governors indeed more at their ease, at the expense of the people. The late rebellion in Massachusetts has given more alarm, than I think it should have done. Calculate that one rebellion in thirteen States in the course of eleven years, is but one for each State in a century and a half. No country should be so long without one. Nor will any degree of power in the hands of government, prevent insurrections....Educate and inform the whole mass of the people. Enable them to see that it is their interest to preserve peace and order, and they will preserve them. And it requires no very high degree of education to convince them of this. They are the only sure reliance for the preservation of our liberty. After all, it is my principle that the will of the majority should prevail. If they approve the proposed constitution in all its parts, I shall concur in it cheerfully, in hopes they will amend it, whenever they shall find it works wrong. This reliance cannot deceive us, as long as we remain virtuous; and I think we shall be so, as long as agriculture is our principal object, which will be the case, while there remains vacant lands in any part of America. When we get piled upon one another in large cities, as in Europe, we shall become corrupt as in Europe, and go to eating one another as they do there....

Th: Jefferson

THE STAR-SPANGLED BANNER

FRANCIS SCOTT KEY, 1814

Oh, say can you see by the dawn's early light
What so proudly we hail'd at the twilight's last gleaming,
Whose broad stripes and bright stars through the perilous fight,
O'er the ramparts we watch'd, were so gallantly streaming?
And the rockets' red glare, the bombs bursting in air,
Gave proof through the night that our flag was still there.
Oh say does that star-spangled banner yet wave
O'er the land of the free and the home of the brave?

On the shore dimly seen through the mists of the deep,
Where the foe's haughty host in dread silence reposes,
What is that which the breeze, o'er the towering steep,
As it fitfully blows, half conceals, half discloses?
Now it catches the gleam of the morning's first beam,
In full glory reflected now shines on the stream:
'Tis the star-spangled banner, oh, long may it wave
O'er the land of the free and the home of the brave!

And where is that band who so vauntingly swore
That the havoc of war and the battle's confusion
A home and a country should leave us no more?
Their blood has wash'd out their foul footstep's pollution.
No refuge could save the hireling and slave
From the terror of flight or the gloom of the grave,
And the star-spangled banner in triumph doth wave
O'er the land of the free and the home of the brave.

Oh, thus be it ever, when freemen shall stand
Between their lov'd home and the war's desolation!
Blest with vict'ry and peace may the heav'n-rescued land
Praise the Power that hath made and preserv'd us a nation!
Then conquer we must, when our cause it is just,
And this be our motto, "In God is our trust."
And the star-spangled banner in triumph wave
O'er the land of the free and the home of the brave!

Apple Pie

Apple Pie was originally created by English settlers as a variation on the English meat pie. I discovered this extraordinary version at *Zin* in Sonoma County, California. Chef Jeff Mall explained that the recipe belonged to his mother, Barbara McBride. It is a perennial on his menu.

Piecrust

2 cups sifted all-purpose flour

1 -teaspoon salt

⅔ cup solid vegetable shortening, chilled

6–8 tablespoons ice water

1. Sift the flour and salt together into a mixing bowl. Cut the vegetable shortening into the flour with a pastry blender (or two knives), until the mixture resembles coarse meal.

2. Sprinkle the ice water in a little at a time, blending it quickly into the dough.

3. Wrap the dough lightly in waxed paper and place it in the refrigerator for 30 minutes.

Pie Filling

5 Gravenstein apples, peeled, cut in half, and sliced $1/2''$ thick

$2/3$ cup sugar

3 tablespoons ground cinnamon

about 2 tablespoons lime juice (1 or 2 limes, juiced)

3 tablespoons "Laird's Apple Jack" apple brandy

$1/2$ stick unsalted butter, diced

1 tablespoon heavy cream

sugar for dusting pie crust

1. Preheat oven to 400° F.

2. Divide the dough in half, roll out the bottom piecrust, and place in a 9″ round pie plate.

3. Place a third of the apples on the piecrust. Sprinkle with a third of the sugar, 1 teaspoon ground cinnamon, 1 tablespoon lime juice, and 1 tablespoon apple brandy. Dot the apples with a third of the diced butter. Repeat, starting with the rest of the apples.

4. Roll out the top piecrust and place over the top of the pie. Crimp the edges together, and poke steam vents in the top of the pie.

5. Brush the top with cream, sprinkle it with sugar, and place the pie on a cookie sheet. Slide it into the preheated oven.

6. Bake at 400° F for 15–20 minutes until filling starts to bubble.

7. Lower the heat to 350° F and cook for 20 minutes more.

Let the pie cool slightly and serve with vanilla ice cream.

Serves 6 to 8.

The Civil War

When anti-slavery president Abraham Lincoln was elected, seven states seceded to form the Confederate States of America, with its own constitution and president, Jefferson Davis. On April 12, 1861 Davis' troops attacked the Union-held Fort Sumter in South Carolina, firing the shots that began the war.

Despite pressure, Lincoln insisted the war was more about preserving the Union than fighting slavery. After the battle at Antietam in September 1862, he reconsidered and issued the Emancipation Proclamation.

The first legal African-American regiment was the 54th Massachusetts. Many others followed: in all, 179,000 African Americans served in the Civil War.

William Tecumseh Sherman (1820–1891) led 100,000 Union troops through Georgia, leaving destruction in his wake.

Posing as a Confederate sympathizer, Virginian Elizabeth Van Lew passed information to the North. "Crazy Bet" also arranged prison escapes and hid fugitives.

At least 620,000 Americans died fighting the Civil War—that's more than in all wars America's fought since then, combined.

The Battle of Gettsyburg was the bloodiest of the war. Approximately 23,000 Union and 28,000 Confederate soldiers died before the North declared victory.

Other major battles included Shiloh (24,000 killed) in April 1862, Second Manassas (25,000 killed) in August 1862, Chancellorsville (30,000 killed) in May 1863, and The Battle of the Wilderness (25,000 killed) in May 1864.

The Civil War ended on April 9, 1865, with the Confederates' surrender at Appomattox, in Virginia.

The Civil War created more than 400,000 morphine-addicted veterans.

The Civil War created more than 400,000 morphine-addicted veterans.

Robert E. Lee (1807–1870) commanded the Confederate forces. He led victories at Bull Run, Fredericksburg and Chancellorsville, before surrendering at Appomattox.

Confederate President Jefferson Davis (1808–1889) was a congressman, war hero and secretary of war. He lost his citizenship after the war.

Ulysses S. Grant's (1822–1885) controversial leadership of the Union army caused heavy losses but won the war. He negotiated the South's surrender, and—as our 18th president— presided over the reconstruction.

Confederate commander Thomas J. "Stonewall" Jackson (1824–1863) gained his nickname organizing troops into a line which withstood the Union assault at Bull Run. He died of injuries accidentally inflicted by his own men.

BESORE MEMORIAL LIBRARY
305 E. BALTIMORE ST.
GREENCASTLE, PA 17225

The Gettysburg Address

Abraham Lincoln
Gettysburg, Pennsylvania, November 19, 1863

FOUR SCORE AND SEVEN YEARS AGO our fathers brought forth on this continent a new nation, conceived in liberty, and dedicated to the proposition that all men are created equal.

Now we are engaged in a great civil war, testing whether that nation or any nation so conceived and so dedicated can long endure. We are met on a great battle-field of that war. We have come to dedicate a portion of that field as a final resting place for those who here gave their lives that that nation might live. It is altogether fitting and proper that we should do this.

But in a larger sense, we cannot dedicate—we can not consecrate, we can not hallow—this ground. The brave men, living and dead, who struggled here, have consecrated it, far above our poor power to add or detract. The world will little note nor long remember what we say here, but it can never forget what they did here. It is for us the living, rather, to be dedicated here to the unfinished work which they who fought here have thus far so nobly advanced. It is rather for us to be here dedicated to the great task remaining before us—that from these honored dead we take increased devotion to that cause for which they gave the last full measure of devotion—that we here highly resolve that these dead shall not have died in vain— that this nation under God, shall have a new birth of freedom—and that government of the people, by the people, for the people shall not perish from the earth.

YANKEE DOODLE

Anonymous, 1775

Father and I went down to camp
Along with Captain Goodwin,
And there we saw the men and boys
As thick as hasty pudding.

Chorus
   Yankee Doodle, keep it up,
   Yankee Doodle dandy!
   Mind the music and the steps,
   And with the girls be handy!

There was Captain Washington
Upon a slapping stallion,
Giving orders to his men,
I guess there was a million.

And there they had a swamping gun
As big as a log of maple,

On a deuced little cart,
A load for father's cattle.

And every time they fired it off,
It took a horn of powder;
It made a noise like father's gun,
Only a nation louder.

And there I saw a little keg,
Its heads were made of leather—
They knocked upon it with little sticks
To call the folks together.

The troopers, too, would gallop up
And fire right in our faces,
It scared me almost half to death
To see them run such races.

But I can't tell you half I saw;
They kept up such a smother,
So I took off my hat, made a bow,
And scampered home to mother.

THE PLEDGE OF ALLEGIANCE

OFFICIALLY ADOPTED ON FLAG DAY, JUNE 14 1924
("UNDER GOD" AMENDMENT MADE BY CONGRESS IN 1954)

I pledge allegiance to the flag
of the United States of America
and to the republic for which it stands;
one nation under God, indivisible,
with liberty and justice for all.

African Americans

Born Isabella Baumfree, Sojourner Truth (1797–1883) was a New York slave freed when the state abolished slavery in 1828. She walked throughout the country speaking against slavery.

✴

Frederick Douglass (1818–1895) was an escaped slave whose speeches were instrumental in the issuance of the Emancipation Proclamation.

✴

Harriet Tubman (1820–1913) was a crucial figure in the Underground Railroad; an escaped slave herself, she risked her life to help bring more than 300 slaves into Canada.

✴

Former slave Booker T. Washington (1856–1915) became a prominent educator and orator. In his position as

advisor to two presidents, he was an early advocate of black self-reliance.

✴

W. E. B. DuBois (1863–1963) was the first black to get a Ph.D. from Harvard. He later co-founded the National Association for the Advancement of Colored People (NAACP).

✴

Edward Kennedy "Duke" Ellington (1899–1974) was a pianist, composer, bandleader and musical arranger who defined the sound of jazz with his complex and swinging melodies.

*

Thurgood Marshall (1908–1993) successfully argued the landmark *Brown v. Board of Education* for the NAACP. He went on to become the first African American Supreme Court Justice.

*

By refusing to give her bus seat to a white man in 1955, Rosa Parks (1913–) became the embodiment of resistance to the South's Jim Crow laws. Her gesture sparked a bus boycott that galvanized the civil rights movement.

*

In 1950 Gwendolyn Brooks (1917–2000) became the first black to win a Pulitzer Prize for her poetry collection, *Annie Allen*.

*

Known as the "First Lady of Song," Ella Fitzgerald's (1918–1996) interpretations defined the great jazz composers. She was also a visionary in the art of scat-singing—playing her voice like an instrument, with impeccable rhythm and pitch.

*

After a brief prison term, Malcolm Little became Malcolm X (1925–1965)—a leader of the Nation of Islam who preached black unity and empowerment. In 1964, he converted to orthodox Islam. He was assassinated by former Nation of Islam comrades a year later.

*

The Reverend Martin Luther King, Jr. (1929–1968) was an inspiring civil rights leader. He won the 1964 Nobel Peace Prize for advocating non-violence as the path to social change.

*

Talk show queen Oprah Winfrey (1954–) is one of the richest people in America. The award-winning media mogul and philanthropist also acts, edits her own magazine and produces films.

FROM
RENASCENCE

EDNA ST. VINCENT MILLAY, 1917

All I could see from where I stood
Was three long mountains and a wood;
I turned and looked another way,
And saw three islands in a bay.
So with my eyes I traced the line
Of the horizon, thin and fine,
Straight around till I was come
Back to where I'd started from;
And all I saw from where I stood
Was three long mountains and a wood.

Over these things I could not see:
These were the things that bounded me.
And I could touch them with my hand,
Almost, I thought, from where I stand.

And all at once things seemed so small
My breath came short, and scarce at all.
But, sure, the sky is big, I said:
Miles and miles above my head;
So here upon my back I'll lie
And look my fill into the sky.
And so I looked, and after all,
The sky was not so very tall.
The sky, I said, must somewhere stop.
And—sure enough!—I see the top!
The sky, I thought, is not so grand;
I'most could touch it with my hand!
And reaching up my hand to try,
I screamed to feel it touch the sky.

FROM
ADVENTURES OF HUCKLEBERRY FINN

MARK TWAIN, 1885

WE HAD MOUNTAINS on the Missouri shore and heavy timber on the Illinois side, and the channel was down the Missouri shore at that place, so we warn't afraid of anybody running across us. We laid there all day and watched the rafts and steamboats spin down the Missouri shore, and up-bound steamboats fight the big river in the middle. . . .

When it was beginning to come on dark, we poked our heads out of the cottonwood thicket and looked up, and down, and across; nothing in sight; so Jim took up some of the top planks of the raft and built a snug wigwam to get under in blazing weather and rainy, and to keep the things dry. Jim made a floor for the wigwam, and raised it a foot or more above the level of the raft, so now the blankets and all the traps was out of the reach of steamboat waves. Right in the middle of the wigwam we made a layer of dirt about five or six inches deep with a frame around it for to hold it to its place; this was to build a fire on in sloppy weather or chilly; the wigwam would keep it from being seen. We made an extra steering oar, too, because one of the others might get broke, on a snag or something. We fixed up a short forked stick to hang the old lantern on; because we must always light the lantern whenever we see a steamboat coming down stream, to keep from getting run over; but we wouldn't have to light it for up-stream boats unless we see we was in what they call a "crossing"; for the river was pretty high yet, very low banks being still a little under water; so up-bound boats didn't always run the channel, but hunted easy water.

This second night we run between seven and eight hours, with a current that was making over four mile an hour. We catched fish, and talked, and we took a swim now and then to keep off sleepiness. It was kind of solemn, drifting down the big still river, laying on our backs looking up at the stars, and we didn't ever feel like talking loud, and it warn't often that we laughed, only a little kind of a low chuckle. We had might good weather, as a general thing, and nothing ever happened to us at all, that night, nor the next, nor the next.

Adventures of Huckleberry Finn

Every night we passed towns, some of them away up on black hillsides, nothing but just a shiny bed of lights, not a house could you see. The fifth night we passed St. Louis, and it was like the whole world lit up. In St. Petersburg they used to say there was twenty or thirty thousand people in St. Louis, but I never believed it till I see that wonderful spread of lights at two o'clock that still night. There warn't a sound there; everybody was asleep.

Every night, now, I used to slip ashore, towards ten o'clock, at some little village, and buy ten or fifteen cents' worth of meal or bacon or other stuff to eat; and sometimes I lifted a chicken that warn't roosting comfortable, and took him along. Pap always said, take a chicken when you get a chance, because if you don't want him yourself you can easy find somebody that does, and a good deed ain't ever forgot. I never see pap when he didn't want the chicken himself, but that is what he used to say, anyway.

Mornings, before daylight, I slipped into corn fields and borrowed a watermelon, or a mushmelon, or a punkin, or some new corn, or things of that kind. Pap always said it warn't no harm to borrow things, if you was meaning to pay them back, sometime; but the widow said it warn't anything but a soft name for stealing, and no decent body would do it. Jim said he reckoned the widow was partly right and pap was partly right; so the best way would be for us to pick out two or three things from the list and say we wouldn't borrow them anymore—then he reckoned it wouldn't be no harm to borrow the others. So we talked it over all one night, drifting along down the river, trying to make up our minds whether to drop the watermelons, or the cantelopes, or the mushmelons, or what. But towards daylight we got it all settled satisfactory, and concluded to drop crabapples and p'simmons. We warn't feeling just right, before that, but it was all comfortable now. I was glad the way it come out, too, because crabapples ain't ever good, and the p'simmons wouldn't be ripe for two or three months yet.

We shot a water-fowl, now and then, that got up too early in the morning or didn't go to bed early enough in the evening. Take it all around, we lived pretty high.

World War I

In 1914, tensions already building in Europe came to a head when Archduke Francis Ferdinand of Austria-Hungary was assassinated in Sarajevo by a Serb nationalist. A month later, the world was at war.

America's declared stance of neutrality was severely strained after German subs torpedoed the passenger ship *Lusitania* on May 1, 1915, killing over a thousand people, 123 of them Americans. The tide of public opinion was irreversibly shifted.

Forsaking its own policy of isolationism, America declared war on Germany on April 6, 1917, three years after the war began. The war ended less than a year later.

When the war began, the American air force had just 12 officers, 54 enlisted men and fewer than a dozen planes.

13,000 women (known as Yeomanettes) served with the Navy and Marine Corps in WWI, with the same status as men.

Writers Ernest Hemingway, John Dos Passos, e.e. cummings, W. Somerset Maugham and Dashiell Hammett all served as ambulance drivers during WWI. Gertrude Stein also volunteered medical assistance.

Mustard gas, named for its color and odor, was used later in the war; a blistering agent, it acted with severity on any exposed, moist skin.

WWI innovations—such as trench warfare, tanks and airplanes—changed the way war was fought. Instead of the isolated battles of the past, war was waged on fronts that stretched for miles.

Other WWI inventions included poison gas, first used by the Germans on April 22, 1915, in France. The ensuing five-mile cloud, composed of 168 tons of chlorine gas, resulted in widespread panic and death.

The war's end came at the low point of German resources and morale. Woodrow Wilson's Fourteen Points were accepted as general terms for Germany's surrender on November 11, 1918.

More than 9 million soldiers died in the war. 117,000 of them were Americans.

Best known for having led the first U.S. troops into France, General John Joseph Pershing (1860–1948) held degrees from a teaching academy, West Point and the University of Nebraska's law school. Among his military innovations was the National Guard.

Some 750 poets, playwrights, writers, artists, architects and composers were killed in WWI.

AMERICA

SAMUEL FRANCIS SMITH, 1831

My country, 'tis of thee,
Sweet land of liberty,
Of thee I sing;
Land where my fathers died,
Land of the Pilgrim's pride,
From ev'ry mountainside
Let freedom ring!

My native country, thee,
Land of the noble free,
Thy name I love;
I love thy rocks and rills,
Thy woods and templed hills;
My heart with rapture thrills,
Like that above.

Let music swell the breeze,
And ring from all the trees
Sweet freedom's song.
Let mortal tongues awake;
Let all that breathe partake;
Let rocks their silence break,
The sound prolong.

Our father's God, to Thee,
Author of liberty,
To Thee we sing.
Long may our land be bright
With freedom's holy light;
Protect us by Thy might,
Great God, our King!

State Capitals

UNITE OR DIE

Olympia ⊙ WASHINGTON

Salem ⊙
OREGON

Helena ⊙ MONTANA

Boise ⊙ IDAHO

WYOMING

NEVADA

⊙ Salt Lake City

Cheyenne ⊙

Sacramento ⊙

⊙ Carson City

UTAH

Denver ⊙

CALIFORNIA

COLORADO

Santa Fe ⊙

ARIZONA

NEW MEXICO

Phoenix ⊙

ALASKA

Juneau ⊙

Honolulu ⊙

HAWAII

Augusta, Ga.

NORTH DAKOTA
Bismarck ★

SOUTH DAKOTA
Pierre ★

MINNESOTA
St. Paul ★

WISCONSIN
Madison ★

MICHIGAN
Lansing ★

MAINE
Augusta ★

Montpelier ★
NEW HAMPSHIRE
VERMONT
Concord ★
Boston ★
MASSACHUSETTS

NEBRASKA
Lincoln ★

IOWA
Des Moines ★

ILLINOIS
Springfield ★

INDIANA
Indianapolis ★

OHIO
Columbus ★

Albany ★
NEW YORK
Providence ★
RHODE ISLAND
Hartford ★
CONNECTICUT

KANSAS
Topeka ★

MISSOURI
Jefferson City ★

Frankfort ★
KENTUCKY

WEST VIRGINIA
Charleston ★

PENNSYLVANIA
Harrisburg ★
Trenton ★
NEW JERSEY
Dover ★
DELAWARE
MARYLAND
Annapolis ★

Richmond ★
VIRGINIA

OKLAHOMA
Oklahoma City ★

ARKANSAS
Little Rock ★

Nashville ★
TENNESSEE

Raleigh ★
NORTH CAROLINA

Columbia ★
SOUTH CAROLINA

Atlanta ★
GEORGIA

TEXAS

MISSISSIPPI
Jackson ★

ALABAMA
Montgomery ★

LOUISIANA

Austin ★

Baton Rouge ★

Tallahassee ★

FLORIDA

TES

★ 73

"THE ONLY THING WE HAVE TO FEAR IS FEAR ITSELF"

FRANKLIN DELANO ROOSEVELT
WASHINGTON, D. C., MARCH 4, 1933

In his inaugural address to a nation still reeling from the Great Depression, Franklin Delano Roosevelt conveyed a bold sense of hope and a steely resolve.

THIS IS A DAY OF NATIONAL CONSECRATION, and I am certain that my fellow-Americans expect that on my induction into the Presidency I will address them with a candor and a decision which the present situation of our nation impels.

This is preeminently the time to speak the truth, the whole truth, frankly and boldly. Nor need we shrink from honestly facing conditions in our country today. This great nation will endure as it has endured, will revive and will prosper.

So first of all let me assert my firm belief that the only thing we have to fear is fear itself—nameless, unreasoning, unjustified terror which paralyzes needed efforts to convert retreat into advance.

In every dark hour of our national life a leadership of frankness and vigor has met with that understanding and support of the people themselves which is essential to victory. I am convinced that you will again give that support to leadership in these critical days.

In such a spirit on my part and on yours we face our common difficulties. They concern, thank God, only material things. Values have shrunken to fantastic levels; taxes have risen; our ability to pay has fallen; government of all kinds is faced by serious curtailment of income; the means of exchange are frozen in the currents of trade; the withered leaves of industrial enterprise lie on every side; farmers find no markets for their produce; the savings of many years in thousands of families are gone.

More important, a host of unemployed citizens face the grim problem of existence, and an equally great number toil with little return. Only a foolish optimist can deny the dark realities of the moment.

Yet our distress comes from no failure of substance. We are stricken by no plague of locusts. Compared with the perils which our forefathers conquered because they believed and were not afraid, we have still much to be thankful for. Nature still offers her bounty and human efforts have multiplied it. Plenty is at our doorstep, but a generous use of it languishes in the very sight of the supply.

Our greatest primary task is to put people to work. This is no unsolvable problem if we face it wisely and courageously.

It can be accomplished in part by direct recruiting by the government itself, treating the task as we would treat the emergency of a war, but at the same time, through this employment, accomplishing greatly needed projects to stimulate and reorganize the use of our natural resources....

Finally, in our progress toward a resumption of work we require two safeguards against a return of the evils of the old order; there must be a strict supervision of all banking and credits and investments; there must be an end to speculation with other people's money, and there must be provision for an adequate but sound currency....

We do not distrust the future of essential democracy. The people of the United States have not failed. In their need they have registered a mandate that they want direct, vigorous action.

They have asked for discipline and direction under leadership. They have made me the present instrument of their wishes. In the spirit of the gift I take it.

In this dedication of a nation we humbly ask the blessing of God. May He protect each and every one of us! May He guide me in the days to come!

World War II

General George S. Patton (1885–1945) was nicknamed "Old Blood and Guts." Commanding the U.S. Third Army in Europe, he won a pivotal battle when he and his men drove the Germans back from France after the D-Day landings.

The U.S. was officially neutral until December 7, 1941, when the Japanese attacked Pearl Harbor. At dawn on Sunday, 360 planes attacked in two waves, sinking 16 ships and killing 2,400 military and civilian Americans.

On December 8, 1941, the U.S. declared war on Japan; similar declarations were made against Germany and Italy three days later.

Bob Hope is the only civilian to be made an "Honorary Veteran" for his work entertaining the troops— "G.I. Bob" traveled 30,000 miles to perform for over one million troops in 1945 alone.

During WWII, The Office of Censorship banned baseball announcers from any mention of weather conditions during their broadcasts for fear that enemies wanting to attack the city would receive valuable information.

Norman Rockwell's *Saturday Evening Post* cover depicting "Rosie the Riveter" (May 29, 1943) epitomized the spirit of the nearly 3 million women who entered war work, replacing men called into the armed forces.

On August 6, 1945, the American bomber *Enola Gay* dropped the first atomic bomb on Hiroshima, Japan, destroying 4.4 square miles. Three days later a second atomic bomb landed on Nagasaki. The two attacks killed and wounded more than 200,000. Japan sued for peace the next day.

✷

Champion chess player Reuben Fine helped the war effort by calculating, on the basis of positional probability, where enemy submarines might surface.

✷

More than 500 native Navajo "talkers" were enlisted by the Marines to serve in the Pacific. Navajo, impossible for the Japanese translate, also saved time because it needed minimal coding.

✷

On April 29, 1945, American troops liberated 27,400 prisoners from the Dachau concentration camp. It's estimated another 50,000 died there.

During wartime sugar rationing, most soda companies scaled back production. Not so 7-UP which, being less sweet, required less sugar. Instead, it cashed in with a national advertising campaign.

✷

It took two surrenders to end WWII. In Europe, Germany surrendered to General Eisenhower on May 7, 1945. But in the Pacific, the Japanese continued fighting until the atomic bomb was dropped, finally surrendering on August 14, 1945.

✷

Of all the Americans who served in the armed forces, 6.6% were killed (407,316) or wounded (670,846).

New England Clam Chowder

There is another version of this chowder, made with a tomato base instead of cream, which goes by the name Manhattan Clam Chowder. The very notion of such a variation is considered a crime in the state of Maine, where they once tried to pass a law against it. Here is the classic recipe.

4 tablespoons butter

2 medium yellow onions, peeled and diced

2 tablespoons white flour

4 cups chicken stock

3 russet potatoes, peeled and diced

4 carrots, peeled and finely diced

1 cup leeks, diced

2 teaspoons fresh thyme leaves

$\frac{1}{4}$ cup chopped fresh parsley

4 cups shucked cherrystone clams, quartered

2 cups clam juice

$\frac{1}{2}$ cup half-and-half

1. Heat the butter in a large, heavy pot and sauté the onions over medium-low heat until translucent, about 10 minutes. Sprinkle flour over the onions and cook for another couple of minutes.

2. Add chicken stock slowly, blending as you go, then add the potatoes, carrots, leeks and herbs. Simmer another 10 minutes.

3. Add the clams and the clam juice, reduce heat to low, cover the pot, and slowly simmer until the potatoes are fork tender (another 15 minutes). Add half-and-half and cook another 5 minutes. Serve with oyster crackers.

Serves 8.

LOBSTER ROLLS

This quintessential New England meal actually originated in Connecticut. You have to serve them on hot dog buns to be authentic. They're perfect on a hot summer afternoon with a tall glass of lemonade, or on a cool evening accompanied by a cup of New England Clam Chowder.

3 tablespoons
mayonnaise

1 teaspoon Dijon mustard

2 teaspoons
diced scallions

2 tablespoons
lemon juice

salt and pepper to taste

cooked and chilled
lobster meat from
two 1 pound lobsters,
cut into small chunks

1/2 cup chopped lettuce
(I like iceberg or romaine)

2 celery ribs,
finely chopped

4 buttered hot dog rolls

1. Mix mayonnaise, mustard, scallions, lemon juice, salt, and pepper. Then add lobster meat, chopped lettuce, and celery.

2. Place open buttered rolls face down in a hot skillet for about one minute to toast.

3. Fill the hot dog rolls, and feast.

Serves 4.

AMERICA THE BEAUTIFUL

KATHARINE LEE BATES. 1913

O beautiful for spacious skies,
   For amber waves of grain,
For purple mountain majesties
   Above the fruited plain!
America! America!
   God shed His grace on thee
And crown thy good with brotherhood
   From sea to shining sea!

O beautiful for heroes proved
   In liberating strife,
Who more than self their country loved,
   And mercy more than life!
America! America!
   May God thy gold refine,
Till all success be nobleness
   And every grain divine!

O beautiful for pilgrim feet,
   Whose stern, impassioned stress
A thoroughfare for freedom beat
   Across the wilderness!
America! America!
   God mend thine every flaw,
Confirm thy soul in self-control,
   Thy liberty in law!

O beautiful for patriot dream
   That sees beyond the years
Thine alabaster cities gleam
   Undimmed by human tears!
America! America!
   God shed His grace on thee,
And crown thy good with brotherhood
   From sea to shining sea!

Women

Pocahontas (1595–1617), daughter of a powerful Powhatan chief, helped improve Indian-settler relations by saving the life of settler John Smith. She later married Englishman John Rolfe and traveled to Britain, where she died of smallpox.

Dolley Madison (1768–1849) was a young widow when she married 43-year-old James Madison. She saved the original drafts of the Constitution and the Declaration of Independence from a White House fire.

Elizabeth Cady Stanton (1815–1902) was a writer and orator; Susan B. Anthony (1820–1906) a tactician and organizer. Together they influenced the legislation granting women property rights and, ultimately, the vote.

Elizabeth Blackwell (1821–1910) was the first American woman to earn a medical degree.

Red Cross founder Clara Barton's (1821–1912) fame grew from her campaign to provide care and medical supplies to wounded Civil War soldiers.

Planned Parenthood founder Margaret Sanger (1879–1966) educated women about birth control, campaigned to make methods available, and suffered censorship, jail and lawsuits.

Elected to the House in 1916, Montanan Jeannette Rankin (1880–1973) was America's first congresswoman.

✸

Devoted to helping others, First Lady Eleanor Roosevelt (1884–1962) campaigned for human, women's, and civil rights, and for the young, the poor and democracy.

✸

Amelia Earhart (1897–1937), the first woman passenger to fly the Atlantic, later flew it solo—in a record 14 hours, 56 minutes. In 1937, she vanished during an attempt to fly around the world.

✸

Colonel Oveta Culp Hobby (1905–1995) was the first female army colonel. Appointed to create a place in the army for women, she led the newly-created Women's Army Corps.

✸

Betty Friedan (1921–) wrote *The Feminine Mystique*, founded the National Organization for Women (NOW) and fought for the Equal Rights Amendment.

✸

Marilyn Monroe (1926–1962) was one of the 20th century's most famous faces. Christened Norma Jeane Baker, she starred in such films as *Some Like it Hot* and *The Misfits*.

✸

Singer Leontyne Price (1927–) debuted at the Metropolitan Opera House in 1961. Her honors include 18 Grammys and the Presidential Medal of Freedom.

✸

First Lady Jacqueline Bouvier Kennedy Onassis (1929–1994), infused the White House with style. After her husband's assassination, she moved to New York with her children and became a book editor.

✸

As a writer, journalist and activist for women's rights, Gloria Steinem (1934–) founded *Ms. Magazine*.

"Ask Not What Your Country Can Do For You"

John F. Kennedy, Washington, D.C., January 20, 1961

At 43, John F. Kennedy was the youngest president elected in U.S. history. In his inaugural address, he called for a patriotic brand of action.

WE OBSERVE TODAY not a victory of party but a celebration of freedom—symbolizing an end as well as a beginning—signifying renewal as well as change. For I have sworn before you and Almighty God the same solemn oath our forebears prescribed nearly a century and three quarters ago.

The world is very different now. For man holds in his mortal hands the power to abolish all forms of human poverty and all forms of human life. And yet the same revolutionary beliefs for which our forebears fought are still at issue around the globe—the belief that the rights of man come not from the generosity of the state but from the hand of God.

We dare not forget today that we are the heirs of that first revolution. Let the word go forth from this time and place, to

friend and foe alike, that the torch has been passed to a new generation of Americans—born in this century, tempered by war, disciplined by a hard and bitter peace, proud of our ancient heritage—and unwilling to witness or permit the slow undoing of those human rights to which this Nation has always been committed, and to which we are committed today at home and around the world.

Let every nation know, whether it wishes us well or ill, that we shall pay any price, bear any burden, meet any hardship, support any friend, oppose any foe to assure the survival and the success of liberty....

In your hands, my fellow citizens, more than mine, will rest the final success or failure of our course. Since this country was founded, each generation of Americans has been summoned to give testimony to its national loyalty. The graves of young Americans who answered the call to service surround the globe.

Now the trumpet summons us again—not as a call to bear arms, though arms we need—not as a call to battle, though embattled we are—but a call to bear the burden of a long twilight struggle, year in and year out, "rejoicing in hope, patient in tribulation"—a struggle against the common enemies of man: tyranny, poverty, disease and war itself.

Can we forge against these enemies a grand and global alliance, North and South, East and West, that can assure a more fruitful life for all mankind? Will you join in that historic effort?

In the long history of the world, only a few generations have been granted the role of defending freedom in its hour of maximum danger. I do not shrink from this responsibility—I welcome it. I do not believe that any of us would exchange places with any other people or any other generation. The energy, the faith, the devotion which we bring to this endeavor will light our country and all who serve it—and the glow from that fire can truly light the world.

And so, my fellow Americans: Ask not what your country can do for you—ask what you can do for your country.

My fellow citizens of the world: Ask not what America will do for you, but what together we can do for the freedom of man.

Finally, whether you are citizens of America or citizens of the world, ask of us here the same high standards of strength and sacrifice which we ask of you. With a good conscience our only sure reward, with history the final judge of our deeds, let us go forth to lead the land we love, asking His blessing and His help, but knowing that here on earth God's work must truly be our own.

Vietnam

American determination to stem the spread of communism in Asia led to direct involvement in Vietnam when the first American "advisors" arrived in 1955.

The U.S. Air Force first deployed the defoliant Agent Orange (named for its orange metal containers) in 1962, in an effort to expose Vietcong trails and roads.

Covert U.S. and South Vietnamese naval operations began in early 1965. "Operation Rolling Thunder"—sustained bombing raids of North Vietnam—began in February and continued for three years.

The first Marines arrived in Danang, Vietnam in 1965.

Protests weren't just for radicals and hippies: as early as 1966, veterans of World Wars I and II and the Korean War rallied in New York against American involvement in Vietnam.

Recruiters from Dow Chemical, the manufacturer of Napalm, were driven from the University of Wisconsin at Madison in 1967, amid massive student protests.

On January 31, 1968, the North Vietnamese launched the surprise Tet Offensive. Though U.S. forces ultimately pushed back the communists, the event revealed how badly America had underestimated the Vietcong.

Charlie Company, 11th Brigade, American Division, slaughtered more than 300 civilians in the village of My Lai on March 16, 1968. A shocked America only learned of the infamous massacre a year later. Commanding officer Lt. William Calley was convicted of murder in 1971.

"Operation Breakfast" was a covert bombing campaign in Cambodia ordered by President Nixon in 1969, without the knowledge of Congress or the American people.

On May 4, 1970, four students were killed and eight others wounded when National Guardsmen opened fire on an antiwar demonstration at Ohio's Kent State University.

The New York Times published the Pentagon Papers in 1971. Leaked from inside the government, they detailed years of deception by the U.S. military and the White House concerning America's policy in Vietnam.

Nixon ordered the demobilization of 70,000 troops 1972. In 1973, Henry Kissinger and North Vietnam's Le Duc Tho signed a cease-fire agreement. Congressional hearings on the bombing of Cambodia resulted in an order to stop all such bombings on August 15, 1973.

The last American troops were evacuated from Saigon in 1975, as the city fell to communist forces.

For the U.S., the war produced more than 2 million veterans, took more than 58,000 lives and cost more than $150 billion.

WILLIAM LEDERER TO
ADMIRAL DAVID McDONALD

1962

William Lederer is the co-author of The Ugly American *(1958), which portrayed the boorish side of Americans overseas. Four years after its publication, he had an experience while traveling in France with his family that prompted his writing to the Chief of U.S. Naval Operations.*

Admiral David L. McDonald, USN
Chief of Naval Operations
Washington, D.C.

Dear Admiral McDonald,

*E*ighteen people asked me to write this letter to you.

Last year at Christmas time, my wife, three boys and I were in France, on our way from Paris to Nice. For five wretched days everything had gone wrong. Our hotels were "tourist traps," our rented car broke down; we were all restless and irritable in the crowded car. On Christmas Eve, when we checked into our hotel in Nice, there was no Christmas spirit in our hearts.

It was raining and cold when we went out to eat. We found a drab little restaurant shoddily decorated for the holiday. Only five tables were occupied. There were two German couples, two French families, and an American sailor, by himself. In the corner a piano player listlessly played Christmas music.

I was too tired and miserable to leave. I noticed that the other customers were eating in stony silence. The only person who seemed happy was the American sailor. While eating, he was writing a letter, and a half-smile lighted his face.

My wife ordered our meal in French. The waiter brought us the wrong thing. I scolded my wife for being stupid. The boys defended her, and I felt even worse.

Then, at the table with the French family on our left, the father slapped one of his children for some minor infraction, and the boy began to cry.

On our right, the German wife began berating her husband....Through the front door came an old flower woman. She wore a dripping, tattered overcoat, and shuffled in on wet, rundown shoes. She went from one table to the other.

"Flowers, monsieur? Only one franc."

No one bought any.

Wearily she sat down at a table between the sailor and us. To the waiter she said, "A bowl of soup. I haven't sold a flower all afternoon." To the piano player she said hoarsely, "Can you imagine, Joseph, soup on Christmas Eve?"

He pointed to his empty "tipping plate."

The young sailor finished his meal and got up to leave. Putting on his coat, he walked over to the flower woman's table.

"Happy Christmas," he said, smiling and picking out two corsages. "How much are they?"

"Two francs, monsieur."

Pressing one of the small corsages flat, he put it into the letter he had written, then handed the woman a 20-franc note.

"I don't have change, monsieur," she said. "I'll get some from the waiter."

"No, ma'am," said the sailor, leaning over and kissing the ancient cheek. "This is my Christmas present to you."

Then he came to our table, holding the other corsage in front of him. "Sir," he said to me, "may I have permission to present these flowers to your beautiful daughter?"

In one quick motion he gave my wife the corsage, wished us a Merry Christmas and departed.

Everyone had stopped eating. Everyone had been watching the sailor. Everyone was silent.

A few seconds later Christmas exploded throughout the restaurant like a bomb.

The old flower woman jumped up, waving the 20-franc note, shouted to the piano player, "Joseph, my Christmas present! And you shall have half so you can have a feast too."

The piano player began to belt out *Good King Wencelaus*, beating the keys with magic hands.

My wife waved her corsage in time to the music. She appeared 20 years younger. She began to sing, and our three sons joined her, bellowing with enthusiasm.

"*Gut! Gut!*" shouted the Germans. They began singing in German.

The waiter embraced the flower woman. Waving their arms, they sang in French.

The Frenchman who had slapped the boy beat rhythm with his fork against a bottle. The lad climbed on his lap, singing in a youthful soprano.

A few hours earlier 18 persons had been spending a miserable evening. It ended up being the happiest, the very best Christmas Eve, they had ever experienced.

This, Admiral McDonald, is what I am writing you about. As the top man in the Navy, you should know about the very special gift that the U.S. Navy gave to my family, to me and to the other people in that French restaurant. Because your young sailor had Christmas spirit in his soul, he released the love and joy that had been smothered within us by anger and disappointment. He gave us Christmas.

Thank you, Sir, very much.

Merry Christmas,
Bill Lederer

The New Colossus

Emma Lazarus, 1883

inscribed on The Statue of Liberty in 1901

Not like the brazen giant of Greek fame,
With conquering limbs astride from land to land;
Here at our sea-washed, sunset gates shall stand
A mighty woman with a torch, whose flame
Is imprisoned lightning, and her name
Mother of Exiles. From her beacon-hand
Glows world-wide welcome; her mild eyes command
The air-bridged harbor that twin cities frame.
"Keep, ancient lands, your storied pomp!" cries she
With silent lips. "Give me your tired, your poor,
Your huddled masses yearning to breathe free,
The wretched refuse of your teeming shore.
Send these, the homeless, tempest-tost to me,
I lift my lamp beside the golden door!"

Washington, D.C.

Irish-American architect James Hoban won a 1792 competition for the design of the White House. After the British attacked and burned the building down to a shell in 1812, Hoban oversaw the restoration.

Telephones outnumber residents in the nation's capital.

Ironically, Washington, D.C.—our nation's capital—has no voting representation in Congress.

There aren't any skyscrapers in Washington D.C. because a city ordinance says the Washington Monument—at 555 feet high—must always be visible.

Construction of the Washington Monument began in 1848 but wasn't completed until 34 years later. Protests over marble donated by Pope Pius IX and succeeding political squabbling stopped work for 26 years. The Monument finally opened to the public in 1888.

Sixty years to the day before terrorists flew a plane into the Pentagon (September 11, 2001), ground was broken in Arlington, Virginia for what was then called "The War Department."

Sprawling over more than 583 acres, the Pentagon is the world's largest office complex.

At George Washington's request, in 1791, the French civil engineer Pierre L'Enfant designed a plan for "Federal City," which would become Washington, D.C. A year later, Washington fired L'Enfant for insisting on complete control of the project.

D.C. became the permanent capital on December 1, 1800. Before that, the seat of government moved among seven different cities: New York, York, Lancaster, Baltimore, Annapolis, Princeton, Trenton and Philadelphia.

There are 132 rooms in the White House, of which 35 are bathrooms. Originally known as the "Executive Mansion," it was dubbed the White House in 1901 by Theodore Roosevelt.

The U.S. Capitol Building, which has no formal address, has 365 steps: one for each day of the year.

ADDRESS TO THE BRITISH PEOPLE

FREDERICK DOUGLASS, MAY 12, 1846

A self-educated slave who escaped in 1838 and headed North, Frederick Douglass became a renowned orator against slavery and was soon traced by his former owner. In the early 1840s he went on a speaking tour of England to raise the funds to buy his freedom.

I DENY THE CHARGE that I am saying a word against the institutions of America, or the people, as such. What I have to say is against slavery and slaveholders. I feel at liberty to speak on this subject. I have on my back the marks of the lash; I have four sisters and one brother now under the galling chain. I feel it my duty to cry aloud and spare not. I am not averse to having the good opinion of my fellow-creatures. I am not averse to being kindly regarded by all men; but I am bound, even at the hazard of making a large class of religionists in this country hate me, oppose me, and malign me as they have done—I am bound by the prayers, and tears, and entreaties of three millions of kneeling bondsmen, to have no compromise with men who are in any shape or form connected with the slaveholders of America. I expose slavery in this country, because to expose it is to kill it. Slavery is one of those monsters of darkness to whom the light of truth is death. Expose slavery, and it dies. Light is to slavery what the heat of the sun is to the root of a tree; it must die under it.... The slaveholders want total darkness on the subject. They want the hatchway shut down, that the monster may crawl in his den of darkness, crushing human hopes and happiness, destroying the bondman at will, and having no one to reprove or rebuke him. Slavery shrinks from the light; it hateth the light, neither cometh to the light, lest its deeds should be reproved. To tear off the mask from this abominable system, to expose it to the light of heaven, aye, to the heat of the sun, that it may burn and wither it out of existence, is my object in coming to this country. I want the slaveholder surrounded, as by a wall of anti-slavery fire, so that he may see the condemnation of himself and his system glaring down in letters of light. I want him to feel that he has no sympathy in England, Scotland, or Ireland; that he has none in Canada, none in Mexico, none among the poor wild Indians; that the voice of the civilized, aye, and savage world is against him. I would have condemnation blaze down upon him in every direction, till, stunned and overwhelmed with shame and confusion, he is compelled to let go the grasp he holds upon the persons of his victims, and restore them to their long-lost rights.

The Emancipation Proclamation

ABRAHAM LINCOLN, JANUARY 1, 1863

Whereas, on the twenty-second day of September, in the year of our Lord one thousand eight hundred and sixty-two, a proclamation was issued by the President of the United States, containing, among other things, the following, to wit:

"That on the first day of January, in the year of our Lord one thousand eight hundred and sixty-three, all persons held as slaves within any State, or designated part of a State, the people whereof shall then be in rebellion against the United States, shall be then, thenceforward, and forever free; and the Executive Government of the United States, including the military and naval authority thereof, will recognize and maintain the freedom of such persons, and will do no act or acts to repress such persons, or any of them, in any efforts they may make for their actual freedom.

"That the Executive will, on the first day of January aforesaid, by proclamation, designate the States and parts of States, if any, in which the people thereof respectively shall then be in rebellion against the United States; and the fact that any State, or the people thereof, shall on that day be in good faith represented in the Congress of the United States by members chosen thereto at elections wherein a majority of the qualified voters of such State shall have participated, shall in the absence of strong countervailing testimony be deemed conclusive evidence that such State and the people thereof are not then in rebellion against the United States."

Now, therefore, I, Abraham Lincoln, President of the United States, by virtue of the power in me vested as commander-in-chief of the army and navy of the United States in time of actual armed rebellion against the authority and government of the United States, and as a fit and necessary war measure for suppressing said rebellion, do, on this first day of January, in the year of our Lord one thousand eight hundred and sixty-three, and in accordance with my purpose so to do, publicly proclaimed for the full period of 100 days from the day first above mentioned, order and designate as the States and parts of States wherein the people thereof, respectively, are this day in rebellion against the United States, the following, to wit:

Arkansas, Texas, Louisiana (except the parishes of St. Bernard, Plaquemines, Jefferson, St. John, St. Charles, St. James, Ascension, Assumption, Terre Bonne, Lafourche, St. Mary, St. Martin, and Orleans, including the city of New Orleans), Mississippi, Alabama, Florida, Georgia, South Carolina, North Carolina, and Virginia (except the forty-eight counties designated as West Virginia, and also the counties of Berkeley, Accomac, Northampton, Elizabeth City, York, Princess Ann, and Norfolk, including the cities of Norfolk and Portsmouth), and which excepted parts are for the present left precisely as if this proclamation were not issued.

And by virtue of the power and for the purpose aforesaid, I do order and declare that all persons held as slaves within said designated States and parts of States are, and henceforward shall be, free; and that the Executive Government of the United States, including the military and naval authorities thereof, will recognize and maintain the freedom of said persons.

And I hereby enjoin upon the people so declared to be free to abstain from all violence, unless in necessary self-defense; and I recommend to them that, in all cases when allowed, they labor faithfully for reasonable wages.

And I further declare and make known that such persons of suitable condition will be received into the armed service of the United States to garrison forts, positions, stations, and other places, and to man vessels of all sorts in said service.

And upon this act, sincerely believed to be an act of justice, warranted by the Constitution upon military necessity, I invoke the considerate judgment of mankind and the gracious favor of Almighty God.

SULLIVAN BALLOU TO HIS WIFE SARAH

CAMP CLARK, WASHINGTON, JULY 14, 1861

Major Sullivan Ballou, of the 2nd Rhode Island Volunteers, wrote the following letter to his wife, Sarah, before the battle of Bull Run. The Union army was badly defeated in this first major battle of the war. 4,500 soldiers on both sides were killed, wounded or captured. Major Ballou was among the dead.

My very dear Sarah,

The indications are very strong that we shall move in a few days—perhaps tomorrow. Lest I should not be able to write again, I feel impelled to write a few lines that may fall under your eye when I shall be no more....

I have no misgivings about, or lack of confidence in, the cause in which I am engaged, and my courage does not halt or falter. I know how strongly American Civilization now leans on the triumph of the Government, and how great a debt we owe to those who went before us through the blood and sufferings of the Revolution. And I am willing—perfectly willing—to lay down all my joys in this life, to help maintain this Government, and to pay that debt....

Sarah my love for you is deathless. It seems to bind me with mighty cables that nothing but Omnipotence could break; and yet my love of Country comes over me like a strong wind and bears me unresistibly on with all these chains to the battlefield.

The memories of the blissful moments I have spent with you come creeping over me, and I feel most gratified to God and to you that I have enjoyed them so long. And hard it is for me to give them up and burn to ashes the hopes of future years, when, God willing, we might still have lived and loved together, and seen our sons grown up to honorable manhood around us. I have, I know, but few and small claims upon Divine Providence, but something whispers to me—perhaps it is the wafted prayer of my little Edgar—that I shall return to my loved ones unharmed. If I do not my dear Sarah, never forget how much I love you, and when my last breath escapes me on the battlefield, it will whisper your name. Forgive my many faults, and the many pains I have caused you. How thoughtless and foolish I have often times been! How gladly would I wash out with my tears every little spot upon your happiness, and struggle with all the misfortunes of this world to shield you and your children from harm. But I cannot. I must watch you from the Spirit-land and hover near you, while you buffet the storm, with your precious little freight, and wait with sad patience till we meet to part no more.

But, O Sarah! if the dead can come back to this earth and flit unseen around those they loved, I shall always be near you; in the gladdest days and darkest nights, advised to your happiest scenes and gloomiest hours, *always, always,* and if there be a soft breeze upon your cheek, it shall be my breath; as the cool air fans your throbbing temple, it shall be my spirit passing by. Sarah do not mourn me dead; think I am gone and wait for thee, for we shall meet again.

As for my little boys—they will grow up as I have done, and never know a father's love and care. Little Willie is too young to remember me long, and my blue-eyed Edgar will keep my frolics with him among the dim memories of childhood. Sarah, I have unlimited confidence in your maternal care and your development of their character, and feel that God will bless you in your holy work.

Tell my two Mothers I call God's blessing upon them. O! Sarah. I wait for you there; come to me and lead thither my children.

Sullivan

The Declaration of Independence

IN CONGRESS, JULY 4, 1776

When in the Course of human events it becomes necessary for one people to dissolve the political bands which have connected them with another, and to assume among the powers of the earth, the separate and equal station to which the Laws of Nature and of Nature's God entitle them, a decent respect to the opinions of mankind requires that they should declare the causes which impel them to the separation.

We hold these truths to be self-evident, that all men are created equal, that they are endowed by their Creator with certain unalienable Rights, that among these are Life, Liberty and the pursuit of Happiness. That to secure these rights, Governments are instituted among Men, deriving their just powers from the consent of the governed, That whenever any Form of Government becomes destructive of these ends, it is the Right of the People to alter or to abolish it, and to institute new Government, laying its foundation on such principles and organizing its powers in such form, as to them shall seem most likely to effect their Safety and Happiness....

The Preamble to the Bill of Rights

NEW YORK, 1789

CONGRESS OF THE UNITED STATES
begun and held at the City of New-York, on
Wednesday the fourth of March, one thousand seven hundred
and eighty nine.

THE Conventions of a number of the States, having at the time of
their adopting the Constitution, expressed a desire, in order to prevent
misconstruction or abuse of its powers, that further declaratory and
restrictive clauses should be added: And as extending the ground of
public confidence in the Government, will best ensure the beneficent
ends of its institution.

RESOLVED by the Senate and House of Representatives of the United
States of America, in Congress assembled, two thirds of both Houses
concurring, that the following Articles be proposed to the Legislatures
of the several States, as amendments to the Constitution of the United
States, all, or any of which Articles, when ratified by three fourths of

the said Legislatures, to be valid to all intents and purposes, as part of the said Constitution; viz.

ARTICLES in addition to, and Amendment of the Constitution of the United States of America, proposed by Congress, and ratified by the Legislatures of the several States, pursuant to the fifth Article of the original Constitution.

AMENDMENT I
Congress shall make no law respecting an establishment of religion, or prohibiting the free exercise thereof; or abridging the freedom of speech, or of the press; or the right of the people peaceably to assemble, and to petition the Government for a redress of grievances.

AMENDMENT II
A well regulated Militia, being necessary to the security of a free State, the right of the people to keep and bear Arms, shall not be infringed.

AMENDMENT III
No Soldier shall, in time of peace be quartered in any house, without the consent of the Owner, nor in time of war, but in a manner to be prescribed by law.

AMENDMENT IV
The right of the people to be secure in their persons, houses, papers, and effects, against unreasonable searches and seizures, shall not be violated, and no Warrants shall issue, but upon probable cause,

supported by Oath or affirmation, and particularly describing the place to be searched, and the persons or things to be seized.

AMENDMENT V

No person shall be held to answer for a capital, or otherwise infamous crime, unless on a presentment or indictment of a Grand Jury, except in cases arising in the land or naval forces, or in the Militia, when in actual service in time of War or public danger; nor shall any person be subject for the same offence to be twice put in jeopardy of life or limb; nor shall be compelled in any criminal case to be a witness against himself, nor be deprived of life, liberty, or property, without due process of law; nor shall private property be taken for public use, without just compensation.

AMENDMENT VI

In all criminal prosecutions, the accused shall enjoy the right to a speedy and public trial, by an impartial jury of the State and district wherein the crime shall have been committed, which district shall have been previously ascertained by law, and to be informed of the nature and cause of the accusation; to be confronted with the witnesses against him; to have compulsory process for obtaining witnesses in his favor, and to have the Assistance of Counsel for his defense.

AMENDMENT VII

In suits at common law, where the value in controversy shall exceed twenty dollars, the right of trial by jury shall be preserved, and no fact tried by a jury, shall be otherwise reexamined in any Court of the United States, than according to the rules of the common law.

AMENDMENT VIII

Excessive bail shall not be required, nor excessive fines imposed, nor cruel and unusual punishments inflicted.

AMENDMENT IX

The enumeration in the Constitution, of certain rights, shall not be construed to deny or disparage others retained by the people.

AMENDMENT X

The powers not delegated to the United States by the Constitution, nor prohibited by it to the States, are reserved to the States respectively, or to the people.

AMENDMENT XI

Passed by Congress March 4, 1794. Ratified February 7, 1795.
The Judicial power of the United States shall not be construed to extend to any suit in law or equity, commenced or prosecuted against one of the United States by Citizens of another State, or by Citizens or Subjects of any Foreign State.

AMENDMENT XII

Passed by Congress December 9, 1803. Ratified June 15, 1804.
The Electors shall meet in their respective states and vote by ballot for President and Vice-President, one of whom, at least, shall not be an

inhabitant of the same state with themselves; they shall name in their ballots the person voted for as President, and in distinct ballots the person voted for as Vice-President, and they shall make distinct lists of all persons voted for as President, and of all persons voted for as Vice-President, and of the number of votes for each, which lists they shall sign and certify, and transmit sealed to the seat of the government of the United States, directed to the President of the Senate;—the President of the Senate shall, in the presence of the Senate and House of Representatives, open all the certificates and the votes shall then be counted;—The person having the greatest number of votes for President, shall be the President, if such number be a majority of the whole number of Electors appointed; and if no person have such majority, then from the persons having the highest numbers not exceeding three on the list of those voted for as President, the House of Representatives shall choose immediately, by ballot, the President. But in choosing the President, the votes shall be taken by states, the representation from each state having one vote; a quorum for this purpose shall consist of a member or members from two-thirds of the states, and a majority of all the states shall be necessary to a choice. [And if the House of Representatives shall not choose a President whenever the right of choice shall devolve upon them, before the fourth day of March next following, then the Vice-President shall act as President, as in case of the death or other constitutional disability of the President.—]* The person having the greatest number of votes as Vice-President, shall be the Vice-President, if such number be a majority of the whole number of Electors appointed, and if no person have a majority, then from the two highest numbers on the list, the Senate shall choose the Vice-President; a quorum for the purpose shall consist of two-thirds of the whole number of Senators, and a majority of the whole number shall be necessary to a choice. But no person constitutionally ineligible to the office of President shall be eligible to that of Vice-President of the United States. *Superseded by section 3 of the 20th amendment.*

AMENDMENT XIII
Passed by Congress January 31, 1865. Ratified December 6, 1865.

SECTION 1.
Neither slavery nor involuntary servitude, except as a punishment for crime whereof the party shall have been duly convicted, shall exist within the United States, or any place subject to their jurisdiction.

SECTION 2.
Congress shall have power to enforce this article by appropriate legislation.

AMENDMENT XIV
Passed by Congress June 13, 1866. Ratified July 9, 1868.

SECTION 1.
All persons born or naturalized in the United States, and subject to the jurisdiction thereof, are citizens of the United States and of the State wherein they reside. No State shall make or enforce any law which

shall abridge the privileges or immunities of citizens of the United States; nor shall any State deprive any person of life, liberty, or property, without due process of law; nor deny to any person within its jurisdiction the equal protection of the laws.

Section 2.

Representatives shall be apportioned among the several States according to their respective numbers, counting the whole number of persons in each State, excluding Indians not taxed. But when the right to vote at any election for the choice of electors for President and Vice-President of the United States, Representatives in Congress, the Executive and Judicial officers of a State, or the members of the Legislature thereof, is denied to any of the male inhabitants of such State, being twenty-one years of age, and citizens of the United States, or in any way abridged, except for participation in rebellion, or other crime, the basis of representation therein shall be reduced in the proportion which the number of such male citizens shall bear to the whole number of male citizens twenty-one years of age in such State.

Section 3.

No person shall be a Senator or Representative in Congress, or elector of President and Vice-President, or hold any office, civil or military, under the United States, or under any State, who, having previously taken an oath, as a member of Congress, or as an officer of the United States, or as a member of any State legislature, or as an executive or judicial officer of any State, to support the Constitution of the United States, shall have engaged in insurrection or rebellion against the same, or given aid or comfort to the enemies thereof. But Congress may by a vote of two-thirds of each House, remove such disability.

Section 4.
The validity of the public debt of the United States, authorized by law, including debts incurred for payment of pensions and bounties for services in suppressing insurrection or rebellion, shall not be questioned. But neither the United States nor any State shall assume or pay any debt or obligation incurred in aid of insurrection or rebellion against the United States, or any claim for the loss or emancipation of any slave; but all such debts, obligations and claims shall be held illegal and void.

Section 5.
The Congress shall have the power to enforce, by appropriate legislation, the provisions of this article.

Amendment XV
Passed by Congress February 26, 1869. Ratified February 3, 1870.

Section 1.

The right of citizens of the United States to vote shall not be denied or abridged by the United States or by any State on account of race, color, or previous condition of servitude—

Section 2.

The Congress shall have the power to enforce this article by appropriate legislation.

Amendment XVI

Passed by Congress July 2, 1909. Ratified February 3, 1913.

The Congress shall have power to lay and collect taxes on incomes, from whatever source derived, without apportionment among the several States, and without regard to any census or enumeration.

Amendment XVII

Passed by Congress May 13, 1912. Ratified April 8, 1913.

The Senate of the United States shall be composed of two Senators from each State, elected by the people thereof, for six years; and each Senator shall have one vote. The electors in each State shall have the qualifications requisite for electors of the most numerous branch of the State legislatures.

When vacancies happen in the representation of any State in the Senate, the executive authority of such State shall issue writs of election to fill such vacancies: *Provided*, That the legislature of any State may empower the executive thereof to make temporary appointments until the people fill the vacancies by election as the legislature may direct.

This amendment shall not be so construed as to affect the election or term of any Senator chosen before it becomes valid as part of the Constitution.

Amendment XVIII
Passed by Congress December 18, 1917. Ratified January 16, 1919. Repealed by amendment 21.

Section 1.
After one year from the ratification of this article the manufacture, sale, or transportation of intoxicating liquors within, the importation thereof into, or the exportation thereof from the United States and all territory subject to the jurisdiction thereof for beverage purposes is hereby prohibited.

Section 2.
The Congress and the several States shall have concurrent power to enforce this article by appropriate legislation.

Section 3.
This article shall be inoperative unless it shall have been ratified as an amendment to the Constitution by the legislatures of the several States, as provided in the Constitution, within seven years from the date of the submission hereof to the States by the Congress.

AMENDMENT XIX

Passed by Congress June 4, 1919. Ratified August 18, 1920.

The right of citizens of the United States to vote shall not be denied or abridged by the United States or by any State on account of sex.

Congress shall have power to enforce this article by appropriate legislation.

AMENDMENT XX

Passed by Congress March 2, 1932. Ratified January 23, 1933.

SECTION 1.

The terms of the President and the Vice President shall end at noon on the 20th day of January, and the terms of Senators and Representatives at noon on the 3d day of January, of the years in which such terms would have ended if this article had not been ratified; and the terms of their successors shall then begin.

SECTION 2.

The Congress shall assemble at least once in every year, and such meeting shall begin at noon on the 3d day of January, unless they shall by law appoint a different day.

SECTION 3.

If, at the time fixed for the beginning of the term of the President, the President elect shall have died, the Vice President elect shall become President. If a President shall not have been chosen before the time

fixed for the beginning of his term, or if the President elect shall have failed to qualify, then the Vice President elect shall act as President until a President shall have qualified; and the Congress may by law provide for the case wherein neither a President elect nor a Vice President shall have qualified, declaring who shall then act as President, or the manner in which one who is to act shall be selected, and such person shall act accordingly until a President or Vice President shall have qualified.

Section 4.

The Congress may by law provide for the case of the death of any of the persons from whom the House of Representatives may choose a President whenever the right of choice shall have devolved upon them, and for the case of the death of any of the persons from whom the Senate may choose a Vice President whenever the right of choice shall have devolved upon them.

Section 5.

Sections 1 and 2 shall take effect on the 15th day of October following the ratification of this article.

Section 6.

This article shall be inoperative unless it shall have been ratified as an amendment to the Constitution by the legislatures of three-fourths of the several States within seven years from the date of its submission.

Amendment XXI

Passed by Congress February 20, 1933. Ratified December 5, 1933.

Section 1.

The eighteenth article of amendment to the Constitution of the United States is hereby repealed.

Section 2.

The transportation or importation into any State, Territory, or Possession of the United States for delivery or use therein of intoxicating liquors, in violation of the laws thereof, is hereby prohibited.

Section 3.

This article shall be inoperative unless it shall have been ratified as an amendment to the Constitution by conventions in the several States, as provided in the Constitution, within seven years from the date of the submission hereof to the States by the Congress.

Amendment XXII

Passed by Congress March 21, 1947. Ratified February 27, 1951.

Section 1.

No person shall be elected to the office of the President more than twice, and no person who has held the office of President, or acted as President, for more than two years of a term to which some other person was elected President shall be elected to the office of President more than once. But this Article shall not apply to any person holding the office of President when this Article was proposed by Congress, and shall not prevent any person who may be holding the office of President, or acting as President, during the term within which this Article becomes operative from holding the office of President or acting as President during the remainder of such term.

Section 2.
This article shall be inoperative unless it shall have been ratified as an amendment to the Constitution by the legislatures of three-fourths of the several States within seven years from the date of its submission to the States by the Congress.

Amendment XXIII
Passed by Congress June 16, 1960. Ratified March 29, 1961.

Section 1.
The District constituting the seat of Government of the United States shall appoint in such manner as Congress may direct:

A number of electors of President and Vice President equal to the whole number of Senators and Representatives in Congress to which the District would be entitled if it were a State, but in no event more than the least populous State; they shall be in addition to those appointed by the States, but they shall be considered, for the purposes of the election of President and Vice President, to be electors appointed by a State; and they shall meet in the District and perform such duties as provided by the twelfth article of amendment.

Section 2.

The Congress shall have power to enforce this article by appropriate legislation.

Amendment XXIV

Passed by Congress August 27, 1962. Ratified January 23, 1964.

Section 1.

The right of citizens of the United States to vote in any primary or other election for President or Vice President, for electors for President or Vice President, or for Senator or Representative in Congress, shall not be denied or abridged by the United States or any State by reason of failure to pay poll tax or other tax.

Section 2.

The Congress shall have power to enforce this article by appropriate legislation.

Amendment XXV

Passed by Congress July 6, 1965. Ratified February 10, 1967.

Section 1.

In case of the removal of the President from office or of his death or resignation, the Vice President shall become President.

Section 2.

Whenever there is a vacancy in the office of the Vice President, the President shall nominate a Vice President who shall take office upon confirmation by a majority vote of both Houses of Congress.

Section 3.

Whenever the President transmits to the President pro tempore of the Senate and the Speaker of the House of Representatives his written declaration that he is unable to discharge the powers and duties of his office, and until he transmits to them a written declaration to the contrary, such powers and duties shall be discharged by the Vice President as Acting President.

Section 4.

Whenever the Vice President and a majority of either the principal officers of the executive departments or of such other body as Congress may by law provide, transmit to the President pro tempore of the Senate and the Speaker of the House of Representatives their written declaration that the President is unable to discharge the powers and duties of his office, the Vice President shall immediately assume the powers and duties of the office as Acting President.

Thereafter, when the President transmits to the President pro tempore of the Senate and the Speaker of the House of Representatives his written declaration that no inability exists, he shall resume the powers and duties of his office unless the Vice President and a majority of either the principal officers of the executive department or of such other body as Congress may by law provide, transmit within four days to the President pro tempore of the Senate and the Speaker of the House of Representatives their written declaration that the President is unable to discharge the powers and duties of his office. Thereupon Congress shall decide the issue, assembling within forty-eight hours for that purpose if not in session. If the Congress, within twenty-one days after receipt of the latter written declaration, or, if Congress is not in session, within twenty-one days after Congress is required to assemble, determines by two-thirds vote of both Houses that the President is unable to discharge the powers and duties of his office, the Vice President shall continue to discharge the same as Acting President; otherwise, the President shall resume the powers and duties of his office.

AMENDMENT XXVI
Passed by Congress March 23, 1971. Ratified July 1, 1971.

SECTION 1.
The right of citizens of the United States, who are eighteen years of age or older, to vote shall not be denied or abridged by the United States or by any State on account of age.

SECTION 2.
The Congress shall have power to enforce this article by appropriate legislation.

AMENDMENT XXVII
Originally proposed Sept. 25, 1789. Ratified May 7, 1992.

No law, varying the compensation for the services of the Senators and Representatives, shall take effect, until an election of representatives shall have intervened.

General Robert E. Lee to His Army

Headquarters, Army of Northern Virginia
April 10, 1865

On April 9, 1865, Confederate General Robert E. Lee surrendered to Union General Ulysses S. Grant. The following day, he addressed his army.

After four years of arduous service, marked by unsurpassed courage and fortitude, the Army of Northern Virginia has been compelled to yield to overwhelming numbers and resources. I need not tell the survivors of so many hard-fought battles, who have remained steadfast to the last, that I have consented to this result from no distrust of them; but, feeling that valor and devotion could accomplish nothing that could compensate for the loss that would have attended the continuation of the contest, I have determined to avoid the useless sacrifice of those whose past services have endeared them to their countrymen. By the terms of the agreement, officers and men can return to their homes and remain there until exchanged. You will take with you the satisfaction that proceeds from the consciousness of duty faithfully performed; and I earnestly pray that a merciful God will extend to you His blessing and protection. With an increasing admiration of your constancy and devotion to your country, and a grateful remembrance of your kind and generous consideration of myself, I bid you an affectionate farewell.

R. E. Lee, General

OVER THERE

GEORGE M. COHAN, 1917

Johnnie, get your gun, get your gun, get your gun,
Take it on the run, on the run, on the run;
Hear them calling you and me,
Ev'ry son of liberty.
Hurry right away, no delay, go today.
Make your Daddy glad
To have had such a lad.
Tell your sweetheart not to pine,
To be proud her boy's in line.

Chorus
Over there, over there,
Send the word, send the word, over there,
That the Yanks are coming, the Yanks are coming,
The drums rum-tumming everywhere
So prepare, say a pray'r,

Send the word, send the word to beware,
We'll be over, we're coming over,
And we won't come back til it's
    over over there.
Over there.

Johnnie, get your gun, get your gun, get your gun,
Johnnie show the Hun, you're a son of a gun!
Hoist the flag and let her fly,
Like true heroes do or die
Pack your little kit, show your grit, do your bit,
Soldiers to the ranks from the towns and the tanks
Make your mother proud of you,
And to liberty be true.

(Chorus)

Abigail Adams
to John Adams
Braintree, Massachusetts, March 31, 1776

Abigail and John Adams wrote frequently while John was in Philadelphia attending the Continental Congress. Abigail often offered political advice to her husband, and informed him of the state of affairs in wartime Boston. In the letter excerpted here, she wrote to John Adams of her excitement at the prospect of independence.

I feel very differently at the approach of spring to which I did a month ago. We knew not then whether we could plant or sow with safety, whether when we had toiled we could reap the fruits of our own industry, whether we could rest in our own Cottages, or whether we should not be driven from the sea coasts to seek shelter in the wilderness, but now we feel as if we might sit under our own vine and eat the good of the land.

I feel a *gaieti de Coar* to which before I was a stranger. I think the Sun looks brighter, the Birds sing more melodiously, and Nature puts on a more cheerfull countenance. We feel a temporary peace, and the poor fugitives are returning to their deserted habitations.

Tho we felicitate ourselves, we sympathize with those who are trembling least the Lot of Boston should be theirs. But they cannot be in similar circumstances unless pusillanimity and cowardice should take possession of them. They have time and warning given them to see the Evil and shun it. –I long to hear that you have declared an independency–and by the way, in the new Code of Laws which I suppose it will be necessary for you to make, I desire you would Remember the Ladies, and be more generous and favourable to them than your ancestors. Do not put such unlimited power into the hands of the Husbands. Remember, all Men would be tyrants if they could. If particular care and attention is not paid to the Ladies, we are determined to foment a Rebellion, and will not hold ourselves bound by any Laws in which we have no voice, or Representation.

That your Sex are Naturally Tyrannical is Truth so thoroughly established as to admit no dispute, but such of you as wish to be happy willingly give up the harsh title of Master for the more tender and endearing one of Friend. Why, then, not put it out of the power of the vicious and the Lawless to use us with cruelty and indignity with impunity. Men of Sense in all Ages abhor those customs which treat us only as the vassals of your Sex. Regard us then as Beings placed by providence under your protection, and in imitation of the Supreem Being, make use of that power only for our happiness.

Abigail

"I WILL FIGHT NO MORE FOREVER"

CHIEF JOSEPH, NEZ PERCÉ
SNAKE CREEK, MONTANA, OCTOBER 5, 1877

Chief Joseph, leader of the Nez Percé, steadfastly refused the white man's attempts to move his people off their Oregon land and onto a reservation. When the tribe was finally forced to leave, they attempted to escape to Canada. But after travelling more than a thousand miles in bad conditions, they were trapped some thirty miles from the border. Chief Joseph made this speech upon their surrender.

TELL GENERAL HOWARD I know his heart. What he told me before, I have it in my heart. I am tired of fighting. Our chiefs are killed; Looking Glass is dead, Ta-Hool-Hool-Shute is dead. The old men are all dead. It is the young men who say "Yes" or "No." He who led on the young men is dead. It is cold, and we have no blankets; the little children are freezing to death. My people, some of them, have run away to the hills, and have no blankets, no food. No one knows where they are— perhaps freezing to death. I want to have time to look for my children, and see how many of them I can find. Maybe I shall find them among the dead. Hear me, my chiefs! I am tired; my heart is sick and sad. From where the sun now stands I will fight no more forever.

The West

90% of North Dakota is covered with farms, making it America's most rural state.

South Dakota's electoral votes have only gone to the Democratic candidate in four presidential elections.

At the juncture of Colorado, New Mexico, Arizona and Utah, known as the Four Corners, you can literally touch four states at once—one with each limb.

Montana's Roe River is the shortest river in the world, flowing 200 feet between Giant Springs and the Missouri River near Great Falls.

Browning, Montana holds the record for the biggest 24-hour temperature change: on January 23, 1916, the mercury plunged 100 degrees—from 44°F to -56°F.

THROWING THE LASSO

★
Denver, Colorado has an average of 300 days of sunshine a year—more than Miami.

★
Oregon produces more peppermint, blackberries, boysenberries, black raspberries and hazelnuts than any other state.

★
Lake Tahoe, which straddles California and Nevada, is 1,645 feet deep. Sitting high in the Sierra Nevada range, it is the deepest and largest mountain lake in North America.

★
Wyoming's Wind River Reservation is home to some 21,000 Arapaho and Shoshone Indians, and covers more than 2.2 million acres. It's the third-largest reservation in the U.S.

★
Mormons comprise 70% of Utah's nearly 2.25 million residents.

CHILI & CORN BREAD

It was once said of legendary bad boy Billy the Kid that "anybody who eats chili can't be that bad." Popularized on the Texas cattle drives, chili's accompaniment, corn bread, was invented when earlier settlers had to substitute Indian corn meal for wheat in their breads.

Chili

1 cup dry red kidney beans or 3 cups canned cooked beans

1 lb. ground round

2 yellow onions, diced

1 small bottle ketchup

2 cans tomatoes (14.5 ounces each) or 4 cups diced and stewed tomatoes

$^1/_8$ teaspoon cayenne pepper (or more if you like it spicy)

$^1/_8$ teaspoon chili powder (or more if you like it spicy)

salt and pepper to taste

Corn Bread

1 $^1/_2$ cups yellow cornmeal

$^1/_2$ cup all-purpose flour

1 cup buttermilk

1 can (8 ounces) creamed corn

$^1/_2$ cup shredded cheddar cheese

$^1/_2$ teaspoon chili powder

2 tablespoons vegetable oil

2 teaspoons baking powder

1 teaspoon sugar

1 teaspoon salt

$^1/_2$ teaspoon baking soda

2 large eggs, mixed

1. If you are using dry beans, soak them overnight in 3 cups of cold water.

2. Simmer the beans for 1 ½–2 hours on the stovetop until tender.

3. Cook the meat and the onions over a medium-high flame, stirring until the meat is brown, crumbled and cooked through.

4. Add the meat and onions to the beans, along with the ketchup, tomatoes and spices. Transfer to a casserole dish.

5. Heat the oven to 450° F.

6. Mix all the corn bread ingredients together in a large bowl. Stir well until completely blended and pour the batter on top of the chili.

7. Bake for 20 minutes until golden brown and serve with a salad.

Serves 6.

THE AMERICAN

ON A BRILLIANT DAY IN MAY, in the year 1868, a gentleman was reclining at his ease on the great circular divan which at that period occupied the centre of the Salon Carré, in the Museum of the Louvre....

An observer, with anything of an eye for national types, would have had no difficulty in determining the local origin of this un-developed connoisseur, and indeed such an observer might have felt a certain humorous relish of the almost ideal completeness with which he filled out the national mould. The gentleman on the divan was a powerful specimen of an American. But he was not only a fine American; he was in the first place, physically, a fine man. He appeared to possess that kind of health and strength which, when found in perfection, are the most impressive—the physical capital which the owner does nothing to "keep up." If he was a muscular Christian, it was quite without knowing it. If it was necessary to walk to a remote spot, he walked, but he had never known himself to "exercise." He had no theory with regard to cold bathing or the use of Indian clubs; he was neither an oarsman, a rifleman, nor a fencer—he had never had time for these amusements—and he was quite unaware that the saddle is recommended for certain forms of indigestion. He was by inclination a temperate man; but he had supped the night before his visit to the Louvre at the Café Anglais—someone had told him it was an experience not to be omitted—and he had slept none the less the sleep of the just. His usual attitude and carriage were of a rather relaxed and lounging kind, but when, under a special inspiration, he straightened himself, he looked like a grenadier on parade. He never smoked. He had been assured—such things are said—that cigars were excellent for the health, and he was quite capable of believing it; but he knew as little about tobacco as about homoeopathy. He had a very well-formed head, with a shapely, symmetrical balance of the frontal and the occipital development, and a good deal of straight, rather dry brown hair. His complexion was brown, and his nose had a bold, well-marked arch. His eye was of a clear, cold gray, and, save for a rather abundant moustache, he was clean-shaved. He had the flat jaw and sinewy neck which are frequent in the American type; but the traces of national origin are a matter of expression even more than of feature, and it was in this respect that our friend's countenance was supremely

The American

eloquent. The discriminating observer we have been supposing might, however, perfectly have measured its expressiveness, and yet have been at a loss to describe it. It had that typical vagueness which is not vacuity, that blankness which is not simplicity, that look of being committed to nothing in particular, of standing in an attitude of general hospitality to the chances of life, of being very much at one's own disposal, so characteristic of many American faces. It was our friend's eye that chiefly told his story; an eye in which innocence and experience were singularly blended. It was full of contradictory suggestions; and though it was by no means the glowing orb of a hero of romance, you could find in it almost anything you looked for. Frigid and yet friendly, frank yet cautious, shrewd yet credulous, positive yet sceptical, confident yet shy, extremely intelligent and extremely good-humoured, there was something vaguely defiant in its concessions, and something profoundly reassuring in its reserve. The cut of this gentleman's moustache, with the two premature wrinkles in the cheek above it, and the fashion of his garments, in which an exposed shirt-front and a cerulean cravat played perhaps an obtrusive part, completed the conditions of his identity.

Science & Invention

✳

Benjamin Franklin (1706–1790) was an inventor, publisher, writer, statesman, scientist and philosopher. Entirely self-taught, he was also self-made, a former printer's apprentice who became one of America's founding fathers.

✳

By demonstrating that more than 300 products could be made from the peanut, former slave George Washington Carver (1864–1943) revolutionized the agricultural economy of the American south— freeing it from a historic dependency on cotton.

✳

From his New Jersey lab, Thomas Edison (1847–1931) invented many objects that shape our modern world, including the light bulb.

✳

Astronomer Edwin Hubble (1889–1953) discovered that our Milky Way is only one of billions of galaxies and that the universe continues to expand into infinity.

✳

The cotton gin, invented by Eli Whitney (1765–1825) in 1794, was a key development in America's first industrial revolution. It included a device that separated seed from cotton, and it made the South rich.

✳

Alexander Graham Bell (1847–1922) invented the telephone in 1876. His original name for it was an "electrical speech machine."

✳

Wright brothers Wilbur (1867–1912) and Orville (1871–1948)—inveterate tinkerers and bicycle shop-owners—were the first to successfully fly a motorized airplane. Their history-making flight, on December 17, 1903, lasted 12 seconds.

✳

Albert Einstein (1879–1955) was a Swiss patent clerk who, in 1916, developed the ground-breaking theory of relativity known as "e=mc²." Awarded the Nobel Prize in 1921, he later emigrated to America.

✳

Michigan native Henry Ford (1863–1947) set the course of American industrial production with his 1908 invention—a motorized vehicle that could be mass-produced. In the first 19 years, the Ford Motor Company cranked out approximately 10 million Model T's.

✳

Jonas Salk (1914–1995) discovered the antidote for polio in 1954: his vaccine, alternated with booster shots of the vaccine developed by Albert Sabin, effectively eradicated the crippling disease.

✳

Samuel Morse (1791–1872) is best known for inventing the Morse code (1838), a dot-dot-dash system that became indispensable to the military.

✳

In 1975, 19-year-old Harvard dropout Bill Gates (1955–) founded Microsoft; Apple Computers was founded by Steve Wozniak (1950–) and Steve Jobs (1955–) in 1976. Together the two companies revolutionized the world of personal computers.

CITYWIDE PRAYER SERVICE AT YANKEE STADIUM

RUDOLPH GIULIANI, SEPTEMBER 23, 2001

EVEN IN THE MIDST OF THE DARKEST TRAGEDY there are miracles that help our faith to go on. I would like to share one miracle of September 11th with you.

St. Paul's Chapel is one of the oldest and most historic buildings in the City of New York. It was built in 1766, when the surrounding area was still countryside. The Chapel survived our war of independence—including seven years of wartime occupation.

After George Washington was inaugurated the first President of the United States, in New York City on April 30th, 1789, he walked to St. Paul's, and he kneeled down to pray. The pew where he worshipped is still there. Framed on the wall beside it is the oldest known representation of the Great Seal of the United States of America—it's a majestic eagle, holding in one talon an olive branch, proclaiming our abiding desire for peace…and in the other, a cluster of arrows, a forewarning of our determination to defend our liberty. On a banner above the Eagle is written *E Pluribus Unum*, "Out of Many, One."

For the past twenty-five years, the chapel stood directly in the shadow of the World Trade Center Towers. When the Towers fell, more than a dozen modern buildings were destroyed and damaged. Yet somehow, amid all the destruction and devastation, St. Paul's Chapel still stands...without so much as a broken window.

It's a small miracle in some ways, but the presence of that chapel standing defiant and serene amid the ruins of war sends an eloquent message about the strength and resilience of the people of New York City, and the people of America.

We unite under the banner of *E Pluribus Unum*. We find strength in our diversity. We're a city where people look different, talk different, think different. But we're a city at one with all of the people at the World Trade Center, and with all of America. We love our diversity, and we love our freedom.

Like our founding fathers who fought and died for freedom...like our ancestors who fought and died to preserve our union and to end the sin of slavery...like our fathers and grandfathers who fought and died to liberate the world from Nazism, and Fascism, and Communism...the cluster of arrows to defend our freedom, and the olive branch of peace have now been handed to us.

We will hold them firmly in our hands, honor their memory, and lift them up toward heaven to light the world.

In the days since this attack, we have met the worst of humanity with the best of humanity.

New York

George Washington's inauguration took place on April 30, 1789, in New York City. The Big Apple enjoyed a brief stint as the nation's capitol from 1789–1790.

WASHINGTON'S INAUGURATION AS PRESIDENT.

NYC is the largest city in the U.S. According to the 2000 census, 8,008,278 people live in its five boroughs.

The index finger of the Statue of Liberty in New York harbor is eight feet long.

The Empire State Building took 7 million man-hours, 1 year and 45 days (including Sundays and holidays) to build. It changes colors for special occasions and holidays, and its lights are turned off on foggy nights and during bird migration season.

Some famous New Yorkers: Lucille Ball, Steven Spielberg, Mickey Rooney, James Cagney, John D. Rockefeller, Norman Rockwell, Teddy and Franklin Roosevelt and Walt Whitman.

Who was the real Typhoid Mary? She was Mary Mallon, an Irish immigrant cook who infected 22 New Yorkers with typhoid fever from 1900–1907. When she was finally tracked down, she hid behind a row of trashcans. For the sake of public health she was kept in isolation until her death.

New York City's Cathedral of St. John the Divine is the largest Gothic cathedral in the world. Under construction since 1892, the building is still only two-thirds complete.

Four mountain ranges grace New York state's topography: the Adirondack, Catskill, Shawangunk, and Taconic.

There are more Irish in New York City than in Dublin, more Italians than in Rome, and more Jews than in Tel Aviv.

Broadway, one of the world's longest streets, runs 150 miles, from Bowling Green in lower Manhattan to the state capitol in Albany.

The state insect of New York is the ladybug.

America's first vending machines were installed on New York City subway platforms in 1888. They sold chewing gum.

In 1905, Gennaro Lombardi opened the first pizzeria in North America on New York City's Spring Street.

TO THE MACHINE TENDERS UNION

HARRY GLADSTONE
NEW YORK CITY, AUGUST 13, 1898

Harry Gladstone was a 15-year-old immigrant who organized a union for the children working in the factories. Known as "the boy agitator of the East Side," he gave this speech to a crowd of children hours before giving it to The Machine Tenders Union.

FELLOW WORKMEN, I tell you to stick together.

Think about your poor fathers and mothers you have got to support. [Think] of the schools and how you can't go there to get your education, but must spend from 14 to 15 hours a day in a pest-hole, pulling bastings, turning collars and sleeves, and running around as if you were crazy.

If you don't look out for yourselves, who will? You have not had time to grow up, to get strength for work, when you must spend your dearest days in the sweatshop. Think of the way your mothers kiss you, how they love you, and how they shed tears over you, because they see their dear boys treated like slaves.

Try to make a few dollars for them at least. Then you will come home and kiss your mamas and say "Don't cry, dear Mama. Here, I've brought you some money for rent, or for a Sabbath meal."

The only way to get the bosses to pay us good wages is to stick together, so let us be true to our union.

THANKSGIVING DINNER

(TURKEY, STUFFING, GRAVY, GLAZED CARROTS AND CARMELIZED ONIONS)

Turkey, Stuffing and Gravy

1 large bag (14 ounces) Pepperidge Farm Country Style or Herb Seasoned stuffing

¼ cup Italian parsley, minced

2 onions, minced

1 cup chopped walnuts or chestnuts

1 turkey (approximately 14 pounds)

2 lemons with the skin sliced off

1 stick butter

5 cups chicken stock

1 tablespoon white flour

1 teaspoon cornstarch

The first Thanksgiving dinner was in 1621, when Pilgrims invited more than 90 Native Americans to a three-day feast, which included wild turkey and venison. Today the tradition revolves around the turkey. Everybody has a trick for producing the perfect bird. Mine is simple: baste every 15–20 minutes and bake at a relatively low heat—that way you can cook it until it starts to sag and it will never be dry. Add our mashed potatoes to these side dishes, and you're all set!

1. Preheat oven to 450° F.

2. Prepare the stuffing according to package instructions. Add parsley, onions and nuts.

3. Remove gizzard, livers, neck, and anything else in the turkey cavity. Rinse and dry turkey, and rub inside and out with lemons.

4. Slice the stick of butter into thin pieces and place all over the outside of the turkey. Stuff the turkey.

5. Put the turkey into a roasting pan and pour chicken stock around it. Put into the oven and bake for 20 minutes.

6. Turn heat down to 375° F and baste every 15 minutes for just under five hours (20 minutes per pound). If it gets too brown, cover loosely with aluminum foil.

7. Remove the turkey from the oven and let it cool for 20 minutes.

8. Remove as much fat as possible from the pan. Pour $1/2$ cup of the remaining liquid from the turkey pan into a saucepan. Mix in the flour and cornstarch. When smooth, place saucepan on medium heat and stir until thickened.

9. Remove the stuffing from the turkey and carve.

Glazed Carrots

10–12 medium carrots

4 tablespoons butter

1 $1/2$ tablespoons sugar

salt and pepper to taste

1. Peel, trim and dice the carrots.

2. Simmer the carrots in a pot of salted boiling water until tender, and drain.

3. Melt the butter in a skillet over medium heat. Add the sugar and stir until dissolved.

4. Add the carrots and toss in the butter and sugar until thoroughly coated. Season with salt and pepper and cook until heated through.

Caramelized Onions

3 pints pearl onions

6 tablespoons butter

3 tablespoons sugar

1. Peel the onions and place them in a pot of salted boiling water. Simmer until tender, and drain.

2. Melt the butter in a skillet over medium heat. Add the onions, shaking the pan to coat the onions with butter.

3. Sprinkle with sugar and cook until the sugar begins to caramelize. When the onions are brown, serve.

Serves 6 to 8.

MOBY DICK
HERMAN MELVILLE, 1851

NANTUCKET

Nothing more happened on the passage worthy the mentioning; so, after a fine run, we safely arrived in Nantucket.

Nantucket! Take out your map and look at it. See what a real corner of the world it occupies; how it stands there, away off shore, more lonely than the Eddystone lighthouse. Look at it—a mere hillock, and elbow of sand; all beach, without a background. There is more sand there than you would use in twenty years as a substitute for blotting paper. Some gamesome wights will tell you that they have to plant weeds there, they don't grow naturally; that they import Canada thistles; that they have to send beyond seas for a spile to stop a leak in an oil cask; that pieces of wood in Nantucket are carried about like bits of the true cross in Rome; that people there plant toadstools before their houses, to get under the shade in summer time; that one blade of grass makes an oasis, three blades in a day's walk a prairie; that they wear quicksand shoes, something

MOBY DICK

like Laplander snowshoes; that they are so shut up, belted about, every way inclosed, surrounded, and made an utter island of by the ocean, that to their very chairs and tables small clams will sometimes be found adhering, as to the backs of sea turtles. But these extravaganzas only show that Nantucket is no Illinois.

Look now at the wondrous traditional story of how this island was settled by the red-men. Thus goes the legend. In olden times an eagle swooped down upon the New England coast, and carried off an infant Indian in his talons. With loud lament the parents saw their child borne out of sight over the wide waters. They resolved to follow the same direction. Setting out in their canoes, after a perilous passage they discovered the island, and there they found an empty ivory casket,— the poor little Indian's skeleton.

What wonder then, that these Nantucketers, born on a beach, should take

MOBY DICK

to the sea for a livelihood! They first caught crabs and quahogs in the sand; grown bolder, they waded out with nets for mackerel; more experienced, they pushed off in boats and captured cod; and at last, launching a navy of great ships on the sea, explored this watery world; put an incessant belt of circumnavigations round it; peeped in at Behring's Straights; and in all seasons and all oceans declared everlasting war with the mightiest animated mass that has survived the flood; most monstrous and most mountainous! That Himmalehan, salt-sea Mastodon, clothed with such portentousness of unconscious power, that his very panics are more to be dreaded than his most fearless and malicious assaults!

And thus have these naked Nantucketers, these sea hermits, issuing from their ant-hill in the sea, overrun and conquered the watery world like so many Alexanders; parcelling out among them the Atlantic, Pacific, and Indian oceans, as the three pirate powers did Poland. Let America add Mexico to Texas, and pile Cuba upon Canada; let the English overswarm all India, and hang out their blazing banner from the sun; two thirds of this terraqueous globe are the Nantucketer's. For the sea is his; he owns it, as Emperors

MOBY DICK

own empires; other seamen having but a right of way through it. Merchant ships are but extension bridges; armed ones but floating forts; even pirates and privateers, though following the sea as highwaymen the road, they but plunder other ships, other fragments of the land like themselves, without seeking to draw their living from the bottomless deep itself. The Nantucketer, he alone resides and riots on the sea; he alone, in Bible language, goes down to it in ships; to and fro ploughing it as his own special plantation. *There* is his home; *there* lies his business which a Noah's flood would not interrupt, though it overwhelmed all the millions in China. He lives on the sea, as prairie cocks in the prairie; he hides among the waves, he climbs them as chamois hunters climb the Alps. For years he knows not the land; so that when he comes to it at last, it smells like another world, more strangely than the moon would to an Earthsman. With the landless gull, that at sunset folds her wings and is rocked to sleep between billows; so at nightfall, the Nantucketer, out of sight of land, furls his sails, and lays him to his rest, while under his very pillow rush herds of walruses and whales.

Moby Dick

Old Ironsides

Oliver Wendell Holmes, 1830

Ay, tear her tattered ensign down!
  Long has it waved on high,
And many an eye has danced to see
  That banner in the sky;
Beneath it rung the battle shout,
  And burst the cannon's roar;—
The meteor of the ocean air
  Shall sweep the clouds no more.

Her deck, once red with heroes' blood,
  Where knelt the vanquished foe,
When winds were hurrying o'er the flood,
And waves were white below,

No more shall feel the victor's tread,
  Or know the conquered knee;—
The harpies of the shore shall pluck
  The eagle of the sea!

Oh better that her shattered hulk
  Should sink beneath the wave;
Her thunders shook the mighty deep,
  And there should be her grave;
Nail to the mast her holy flag,
  Set every threadbare sail,
And give her to the god of storms,
  The lightning and the gale!

THE MARINES' HYMN

TRADITIONAL, CIRCA 1870s

From the Halls of Montezuma
To the shores of Tripoli
We fight our country's battles
In the air, on land and sea.

First to fight for right and freedom
And to keep our honor clean;
We are proud to claim the title of
United States Marine.

Our flag's unfurled to every breeze
from dawn to setting sun.
We have fought in every clime and place,
where we could take a gun.

In the snow of far off northern lands
and in sunny tropic scenes,
You will find us always on the job,
The United States Marines.

Here's health to you and to our Corps
which we are proud to serve.
In many a strife we've fought for life
and never lost our nerve.

If the Army and the Navy ever look on
heaven's scenes,
they will find the streets are guarded by
United States Marines.

New England

Nuclear Submarines are refitted in Portsmouth, New Hampshire.

New Hampshire resident Levi Hutchins invented the world's first alarm clock in 1787. It was designed to ring only at 4AM.

Maine has 60 lighthouses, including the Portland Head Light, commissioned by George Washington.

Approximately one-third of Maine's population is of French, French-Canadian, or Acadian ancestry; 7% of Maine's population speak French at home.

There are roughly 25,000 moose wandering around Maine.

The tradition of Christmas Eve caroling reputedly began in Boston, Massachusetts, in the late 1800s.

Vermont has the highest ratio of dairy cows to humans—about one cow for every four people (Wisconsin has the largest number of dairy cows, at 1,410,000).

Vermont's skiers log 4 million ski days a year.

The ubiquitous yellow smiley face was invented by commercial illustrator Harvey Ball in Worcester, Massachusetts. He dreamt up the symbol in 1963 for an insurance company's morale-boosting campaign.

In 1957, 265 years after the last "witches" were hung in Salem Village in 1692, the state of Massachusetts issued a formal apology, officially clearing the names of many who had been accused.

Basketball coach William George Morgan invented the sport of mintonette in Holyoke, Massachusetts in 1895. He later renamed it volleyball.

The praying mantis is the official state insect of Connecticut.

The oldest synagogue in North America is Newport, Rhode Island's Touro Synagogue, founded in 1763.

Massachusetts passed the nation's first law against smoking in public in 1632. The concern was a moral one, however, and had nothing to do with health.

The original Thanksgiving feast could have included cranberry sauce—Massachusetts yields the country's biggest cranberry crop. (The official state beverage is cranberry juice, too.)

Rhode Island's motto is simply: "Hope."

America's first hamburger was served at Louie's Lunch in New Haven, Connecticut in 1895.

AUNT MIMI'S
BLUEBERRY TOP HATS

My dear friend Nancy's Aunt Mimi made these muffins for her as a child, and now, 40 years later, everyone still thinks about them.

6 tablespoons butter

1 cup sugar

2 eggs

1 teaspoon vanilla

2 cups all-purpose flour

2 teaspoons baking powder

$1/2$ teaspoon salt

2 $1/2$ cups blueberries (not rinsed!)

$1/2$ cup milk

2 teaspoons sugar mixed with $1/2$ teaspoon cinnamon for the top

1. Preheat oven to 375° F.

2. Cream butter and sugar well. Add eggs, one at a time, and vanilla, beating well.

3. Sift and mix dry ingredients. Add to wet ingredients, alternating with milk, stirring just to blend.

4. Mash $1/2$ cup of berries and quickly stir into batter. Add rest of berries whole.

5. Grease muffin pan, including entire top surface. Pile batter high to make 12 large muffins. Sprinkle sugar/cinnamon on top.

6. Bake for 25–30 minutes. Let cool for 30 minutes before removing from pan.

Serves 12.

The Road Not Taken

Robert Frost, 1916

Two roads diverged in a yellow wood,
And sorry I could not travel both
And be one traveler, long I stood
And looked down one as far as I could
To where it bent in the undergrowth;

Then took the other, as just as fair,
And having perhaps the better claim,
Because it was grassy and wanted wear;
Though as for that, the passing there
Had worn them really about the same,

And both that morning equally lay
In leaves no step had trodden black.
Oh, I kept the first for another day!
Yet knowing how way leads on to way,
I doubted if I should ever come back.

I shall be telling this with a sigh
Somewhere ages and ages hence:
Two roads diverged in a wood, and I—
I took the one less traveled by,
And that has made all the difference.

Odd Town Names

Humptulips
WASHINGTON
MONTANA
Beer Bottle Crossing
OREGON
IDAHO
WYOMING
Jackpot
Chugwater
Rough and Ready
NEVADA
UTAH
Climax
CALIFORNIA
COLORAD
Dunmovin
Mexican Hat
ARIZONA
Hellhole Palms
NEW MEXICO
Truth or Consequences
ALASKA
Eek
HAWAII

Augusta, Ga.

NORTH DAKOTA

Nimrod

MINNESOTA

SOUTH DAKOTA

Porcupine

NEBRASKA

IOWA

What Cheer

Normal

ILLINOIS   INDIANA

KANSAS

MISSOURI

Buttermilk   Enough

Okay

OKLAHOMA

Toad Suck

ARKANSAS

Noodle   Darling

TEXAS   MISSISSIPPI

LOUISIANA

MICHIGAN

WISCONSIN

Bad Axe
Cat Elbow Corner

MAINE

Lost Nation

Mosquitoville

NEW
HAMPSHIRE   Bald Head

VERMONT

NEW YORK   MASSACHUSETTS   Sandwich

RHODE ISLAND

CONNECTICUT

PENNSYLVANIA

Home

OHIO   NEW
                                          JERSEY   Love Ladies

Blue Ball   Boring   Little Heaven

                   MARYLAND DELAWARE

WEST
VIRGINIA

Surprise   Bumpass

Ordinary   VIRGINIA

KENTUCKY

Difficult   Climax   NORTH
                              CAROLINA

TENNESSEE   Welcome

Between

GEORGIA   SOUTH
                   CAROLINA

ALABAMA

Burnt Corn

Sopchoppy

FLORIDA

TESI

181

FROM
LEAVES OF GRASS
WALT WHITMAN, 1855

I AM OF OLD AND YOUNG, OF THE FOOLISH AS MUCH AS THE WISE,

REGARDLESS OF OTHERS, EVER REGARDFUL OF OTHERS,

MATERNAL AS WELL AS PATERNAL, A CHILD AS WELL AS A MAN,

STUFF'D WITH THE STUFF THAT IS COARSE AND STUFF'D WITH THE STUFF THAT IS FINE,

ONE OF THE NATION OF MANY NATIONS, THE SMALLEST THE SAME
   AND THE LARGEST THE SAME,

A SOUTHERNER SOON AS A NORTHERNER, A PLANTER NONCHALANT AND HOSPITABLE
   DOWN BY THE OCONEE I LIVE,

A YANKEE BOUND MY OWN WAY READY FOR TRADE, MY JOINTS THE LIMBEREST JOINTS
   ON EARTH AND THE STERNEST JOINTS ON EARTH,

A KENTUCKIAN WALKING THE VALE OF THE ELKHORN IN MY DEER-SKIN LEGGINGS,
   A LOUISIANIAN OR GEORGIAN,

A BOATMAN OVER LAKES OR BAYS OR ALONG COASTS, A HOOSIER, BADGER, BUCKEYE;

AT HOME ON KANADIAN SNOW-SHOES OR UP IN THE BUSH,
   OR WITH FISHERMEN OFF NEWFOUNDLAND,

AT HOME IN THE FLEET OF ICE-BOATS, SAILING WITH THE REST AND TACKING,

AT HOME ON THE HILLS OF VERMONT OR IN THE WOODS OF MAINE, OR THE TEXAN RANCH,

Comrade of Californians, comrade of free North-Westerners,
  (loving their big proportions,)
Comrade of raftsmen and coalmen, comrade of all who shake hands
  and welcome to drink and meat,
A learner with the simplest, a teacher of the thoughtfullest,
A novice beginning yet experient of myriads of seasons,
Of every hue and caste am I, of every rank and religion,
A farmer, mechanic, artist, gentleman, sailor, Quaker,
Prisoner, fancy-man, rowdy, lawyer, physician, priest.

I resist any thing better than my own diversity,
Breathe the air but leave plenty after me,
And am not stuck up, and am in my place.

(The moth and the fish-eggs are in their place,
The bright suns I see and the dark suns I cannot see are in their place,
The palpable is in its place and the impalpable is in its place.)

"Are Women Persons?"

Susan B. Anthony, June 1873

In the 1872 presidential election, Susan B. Anthony was arrested and fined for voting illegally, along with a group of women. The incident served well to publicize her cause, which she defended in public speeches.

FRIENDS AND FELLOW CITIZENS, I stand before you tonight under indictment for the alleged crime of having voted at the last presidential election, without having a lawful right to vote. It shall be my work this evening to prove to you that in thus voting, I not only committed no crime but, instead, simply exercised my citizen's rights, guaranteed to me and all United States citizens by the National Constitution, beyond the power of any State to deny....

The preamble of the federal Constitution says:

"We, the people of the United States, in order to form a more perfect union, establish justice, insure domestic tranquillity, provide for the common defense, promote the general welfare, and secure the blessings of liberty to ourselves and our posterity, do ordain and establish this Constitution for the United States of America."

It was we, the people; not we, the white male citizens; nor yet we, the male citizens; but we, the whole people, who formed the Union. And

we formed it, not to give the blessings of liberty, but to secure them; not to the half of ourselves and the half of our posterity, but to the whole people—women as well as men. And it is a downright mockery to talk to women of their enjoyment of the blessings of liberty while they are denied the use of the only means of securing them provided by this democratic-republican government—the ballot....

For any state to make sex a qualification that must ever result in the disfranchisement of one entire half of the people is to pass a bill of attainder, or an ex post facto law, and is therefore a violation of the supreme law of the land. By it the blessings of liberty are forever withheld from women and their female posterity. To them this government has no just powers derived from the consent of the governed. To them this government is not a democracy. It is not a republic. It is an odious aristocracy; a hateful oligarchy of sex; the most hateful aristocracy ever established on the face of the globe;...which makes father, brothers, husband, sons, the oligarchs over the mothers and sisters, the wife and daughters, of every household—which ordains all men sovereigns, all women subjects, carries dissension, discord, and rebellion into every home of the nation....

The only question left to be settled now is: Are women persons? And I hardly believe any of our opponents will have the hardihood to say they are not. Being persons, then, women are citizens; and no state has a right to make any law, or to enforce any old law, that shall abridge their privileges or immunities. Hence, every discrimination against women in the constitutions and laws of the several states is today null and void, precisely as is every one against Negroes....

We no longer petition Legislature or Congress to give us the right to vote. We appeal to women everywhere to exercise their too long neglected "citizen's right to vote." We appeal to the inspectors of election everywhere to receive the votes of all United States citizens as it is their duty to do....

And it is on this line that we propose to fight our battle for the ballot— all peaceably, but nevertheless persistently through to complete triumph, when all United States citizens shall be recognized as equals before the law.

CALAMITY JANE TO HER DAUGHTER, JANEY

SEPTEMBER, 1880

Calamity Jane's daughter was raised by family friends. Though Jane often visited, her daughter never knew her true identity. This letter was part of a journal of letters Jane wrote to her daughter, but never sent.

Janey, a letter from your Daddy Jim came today and another picture of you. Your birthday is this month, you are 7 years old. I like this picture of you…Your expression [is] exactly like your father's….

Your picture brought back all the years I have lived with your Father and recalled how jealous I was of him. I feel like writing about him tonight so I will tell you some things you should know. I met James Butlet Hickock, 'Wild Bill,' in 1870 near Abeline, Kansas. I heard a bunch of outlaws planning to kill him. I couldn't get to where my horse was so I crawled on my hands and knees through the brush past the outlaws for over a mile and reached the old shack where he was staying that night. I told him and he hid me back of the door while he shot it out with them. They hit him, cutting open the top of his head and then they heard him fall and lit matches to see if he was dead. Bill killed them all. I'll never forget what he looked like with blood running down his face while he used two guns. He never aimed and I guess he was never known to have missed anyone he aimed at, I mean wanted to kill, and he only shot in self-defence. Then he was quite sure. I nursed him several days and then while on the trip to Abeline we met Rev. Sipes and Rev. Warren and we were married. There will be lots of fools doubt that but I will leave you plenty of proof that we were. You were not a woods colt Janey. Don't let any of those pusgullied [erased] ever get busy with that lie....

Don't let jealousy get you Janey. It kills love and all the nice things in life. It drove your father from me. When I lost him I lost everything I ever loved except you. I gave him a divorce so he could marry Agnes Lake. I was trying to make amends for the jealous times and my spells of meanness. If she had loved him she would have come out here with him but she didn't and I was glad to have him again even if he was married and she was so far away. I always excused our sin by knowing he was mine long before he was hers. A man can love two women at one time. He loved her and still he loved me. He loved me because of you Janey.

191

California

The California Gold Rush began on January 24, 1848, when gold was accidentally discovered at Sutter's Mill, on the South Fork of the American River in Coloma, near Sacramento.

More people live in California than in any other state in the U.S. In 2001, there were more than 34 million.

The "Eternal God" is a 12,000-year-old redwood tree in the Prairie Creek Redwoods State Park. It's the oldest living thing on the planet, but at 238 feet tall it isn't the biggest tree. That title belongs to a giant sequoia called "General Sherman" in Sequoia National Park, which tops out at 275 feet and measures more than 102 feet around.

Some San Francisco originals: blue jeans and fortune cookies.

The San Andreas fault line runs 650 miles up the California coast, marking the collision of the Pacific and North American tectonic plates. Thousands of small earthquakes occur in California every year; historically, a major quake has hit the southern region every 150 years. The last big one hit in 1857.

Hollywood began in 1908, when a few independent New York filmmakers moved west to set up shop. The town's first full-length motion picture was filmed in 1915.

East finally met west in 1869, when the Central Pacific and Union Pacific railroads were connected.

The hottest day ever in America was in California's Death Valley on July 10, 1913. It was a sweltering 135°F!

Hewlett-Packard was the first tech company in Silicon Valley. In 1938, Stanford University engineers Bill Hewlett and Dave Packard started it in a garage with $1,538.

Los Angeles is moving eastward at an estimated rate of one-fifth of an inch per year.

Mel Blanc, the voice behind Bugs Bunny and Porky Pig, is buried in Hollywood Memorial Park. His headstone reads, "That's all, folks!"

Each October, Pacific Grove, California, becomes home to thousands of Monarch butterflies, who travel up to 2,000 miles to winter and mate there. It's been a misdemeanor to harm a Monarch in Pacific Grove since 1939.

California's stint as a republic, after declaring freedom from Mexico on June 14, 1846, lasted one month. It then spent four years as a U.S. territory before officially becoming a state on September 9, 1850.

AMAZING GRACE

Traditional Hymn, 1760

Amazing grace, how sweet the sound
That saved a wretch like me
I once was lost, but now I'm found;
Was blind, but now I see.

Through many dangers, toils and snares
I have already come
It's Grace that brought me safe thus far,
And Grace will lead me home.

When we've been there a thousand years
Bright shining as the sun
We've no less days to sing God's praise
Than when we've first begun.

"If by Whiskey"

Noah S. Sweat, Mississippi, 1948

Although Prohibition had been repealed, it was still a big political issue in Mississippi in 1948, when Noah Sweat was campaigning for the office of state representative in Alcorn County. So Sweat gave a speech intended to appeal to both sides of the issue. He won the election, and went on serve as prosecutor and eventually Judge of the First Judicial District.

MY FRIENDS, I had not intended to discuss this controversial subject at this particular time. However, I want you to know that I do not shun controversy. On the contrary, I will take a stand on any issue at any time, regardless of how fraught with controversy it might be. You have asked me how I feel about whisky. All right, here is how I feel about whisky.

If when you say "whisky" you mean the devil's brew, the poison scourge, the bloody monster that defiles innocence, dethrones reason, destroys the home, creates misery and poverty, yea, literally takes the bread from the mouths of little children; if you mean the evil drink that topples the Christian man and woman from the pinnacle of righteous, gracious living into the bottomless pit of degradation, and despair, and shame, and helplessness, and hopelessness—then certainly I am against it.

But, if when you say "whisky" you mean the oil of conversation, the philosophic wine, the ale that is consumed when good fellows get together, that puts a song in their hearts and laughter on their lips, and the warm glow of contentment in their eyes; if you mean Christmas cheer; if you mean the stimulating drink that puts the spring into the old gentleman's step on a frosty, crispy morning; if you mean the drink that enables a man to magnify his joy, and his happiness, and to forget, if only for a little while, life's great tragedies, and heartaches, and sorrows; if you mean that drink the sale of which pours into our treasuries untold millions of dollars, which are used to provide tender care for our little crippled children, our blind, our deaf, our dumb, our pitiful aged and infirm; to build highways and hospitals and schools—then certainly I am for it.

This is my stand. I will not retreat from it. I will not compromise.

SOUTHERN FRIED CHICKEN
WITH CREAM GRAVY

The first recipe for this dish was published in *Virginia House-Wife* in 1828. When I was a child there was a magnificent Southern cook who once made Southern fried chicken with paprika in my mother's kitchen. I have spent years trying to recreate that chicken. Crisco was definitely one of the magic ingredients. Goes great with our mashed potatoes.

1 chicken, 3–4 pounds, cut into pieces

2 cups buttermilk

1 ½ cups all-purpose flour

2 tablespoons sea salt or 1 ½ teaspoons salt

¾ teaspoon pepper

2 tablespoons paprika

2 cups Crisco oil

½ cup bacon fat

2 cups milk

1. Coat the chicken with buttermilk in a bowl; cover and chill 6–8 hours.

2. Drain the chicken pieces, discarding the buttermilk.

3. Put ¾ cup flour, 1 teaspoon salt, ½ teaspoon pepper, and 2 tablespoons paprika in a big resealable plastic bag.

4. Heat the oil and bacon fat in a cast-iron or other heavy pot to 360° F (a medium boil). I like the sides of the pot to be high to reduce spatter.

5. Put the chicken pieces into the bag, a couple at a time, and shake until completely covered. Working in batches (the pieces shouldn't be

touching in the skillet) and using tongs, fry the chicken slowly until cooked through and a deep golden brown. Cook several minutes on each side, then turn them occasionally until they have cooked for 25–30 minutes. Keep them warm in the oven while you finish.

6. Drain the chicken pieces on paper towels, leaving $1/4$ cup of the drippings in the skillet.

7. Add $1/4$ cup flour to the drippings and cook, whisking constantly, over medium heat, until the gravy is golden brown.

8. Add milk gradually; cook, whisking constantly, for 3–5 minutes or until thickened and bubbly. Stir in the remaining $1/2$ teaspoon salt and remaining $1/4$ teaspoon pepper, and serve immediately.

Serves 4.

The Midwest

Our quintet of Great Lakes—
Lake Superior, Lake Michigan,
Lake Huron, Lake Erie
and Lake Ontario—holds 18%
of the world's fresh water.

More than 6,000 wrecked
ships can be found at the
bottom of the Great Lakes.

Michigan borders four
of the five Great Lakes.
It gets its name from
the Native American word
michigana, which
means "great or large lake."

Idaho produces 138 million
pounds of potatoes a year.

The citizens of Hell, Michigan
take great pride in the fact that
in the winter of 1995–96,
Hell actually did freeze over.

Nebraska is the only state to have
a unicameral, or one-house,
legislature. Members are elected
to it without party designation,
and have been since 1937.

The Great Fire of Chicago in 1871 did start at around 9 PM on October 8, in the O'Leary's cow barn. But the enduring legend that Mrs. O'Leary's cow was responsible for leveling the entire city (by kicking over a lantern) has never been proven.

In 1887, Argonia, Kansas elected the first female mayor in the nation: Susanna Salter.

Covering only 36,185 square miles, Indiana is the smallest state west of the Appalachian Mountains (not counting Hawaii).

Many Wisconsin towns bill themselves as the capital of something, including:

GREEN BAY—"The Toilet Paper Capital of the World."

BELLEVILLE—"The UFO Capital of Wisconsin."

BLOOMER—"The Jump Rope Capital of the World."

BOSCOBEL—"The Turkey Capital of Wisconsin."

MONROE—"The Swiss Cheese Capital of the World."

MOUNT HOREB—"The Troll Capital of the World."

SHEBOYGAN—"The Bratwurst Capital of the World."

SOMERSET—"The Inner Tubing Capital of the World."

MEATLOAF WITH GRAVY
AND MASHED POTATOES

Meatloaf has been an American staple since the early 1900s. I have been looking for a great recipe for it most of my life. This is it.

Meatloaf

2 pounds ground round

$^1/_2$ cup yellow onions, diced

2 tablespoons parsley, finely chopped

1 $^1/_2$ tablespoons Worcestershire sauce

1 egg

$^1/_2$ can cream of mushroom soup

1 clove garlic, finely chopped

1 teaspoon salt-free seasoning (like Mrs. Dash Table Blend or Trader Joe's 21 Seasoning Salute)

5 ounces Monterey Jack cheese, divided in half

$^1/_4$ cup ketchup

4 bacon slices

$^1/_4$ cup red wine

Gravy

1 to 2 tablespoons flour

$^1/_4$ cup beef broth

$^1/_2$ can cream of mushroom soup

$^1/_4$ teaspoon sea salt

1. Preheat oven to 350°F.

2. In a large bowl, mix the meat, onions, parsley, Worcestershire sauce, egg, mushroom soup, garlic and seasoning together with your hands.

3. Press the mixture into a flattened circle. Put the two hunks of cheese in the center of the circle and fold the meat into a loaf shape to cover them. Transfer into a medium-size casserole dish so that the meatloaf sits in the middle with room on the sides.

4. Cover the top of the meat with ketchup, lay the bacon strips on top, and pour wine into the bottom of the dish.

5. Bake uncovered for 1 hour. Drain the drippings into a saucepan, return the meatloaf to the oven and broil for 5 minutes, until the bacon is sizzling.

6. While the meatloaf broils, heat the drippings over a medium flame, whisking in as much flour as there are drippings. When the gravy bubbles, whisk in the broth and mushroom soup. Continue stirring until thick (approximately 5 minutes). Season to taste and serve.

Mashed Potatoes

6 baking potatoes, peeled and halved

$^{1}/_{2}$ cup milk

$^{1}/_{4}$ cup heavy cream

1 stick unsalted butter

4 tablespoons chopped parsley

salt and freshly ground pepper to taste

1. Place potatoes in enough lightly salted cold water to cover them. Bring to a boil and cook approximately 15 minutes.

2. Drain when the potatoes are soft.

3. Scald the milk and cream in a medium-size saucepan. Add butter and continue cooking on low heat until melted.

4. Mash the potatoes in their pot. Place over medium heat and gradually pour in the scalded milk, stirring with a wooden spoon. Mix until smooth and creamy.

7. Fold in herbs and seasonings.

Serves 4 to 6.

HOME ON THE RANGE

BREWSTER HIGHLEY, CIRCA 1876

O give me a home where the buffalo roam,
Where the deer and the antelope play.
Where seldom is heard a discouraging word,
And the skies are not cloudy all day.

Chorus
Home, home on the range,
Where the deer and the antelope play.
Where seldom is heard a discouraging word,
And the skies are not cloudy all day.

Where the air is so pure, the zephyrs so free,
And the breezes so balmy and light.
Then I would not exchange my home on the range
For all of your cities so bright.

The redman was pressed from this part of the West,
And he's likely no more to return
To the banks of the Red River, where seldom, if ever,
Their flickering campfires burn.

How often at night when the heavens are bright
With the light from the glittering stars,
Have I stood there amazed, and asked as I gazed,
If their glory exceeds that of ours.

I love the wild flowers in this dear land of ours,
And the curlew I love to hear scream.
I love the white rocks and the antelope flocks
That graze on the mountaintops green.

O give me a land where the bright diamond sand
Flows leisurely down the stream.
Where the graceful white swan goes gliding along,
Like a maid in a heavenly dream.

That I would not exchange my home on the range,
Where the deer and the antelope play.
Where seldom is heard a discouraging word,
And the skies are not cloudy all day.

The South

Arkansas has the nation's only active diamond mine.

In 1836, Alabama became the first state to make Christmas an official holiday.

More than 325 motorcycles, some from as far back as 1904, are on display in North America's largest motorcycle collection, in the Barber Vintage Motorsports Museum in Birmingham, Alabama.

Disney World, in Orlando, Florida, covers 27,000 acres of land.

The rights to South Carolina's state anthem, "Carolina," belong to Michael Jackson.

Gladys Knight almost recorded "Midnight Plane to Houston," but she changed the lyrics at the last minute to "Midnight Train to Georgia" because she was from the Peach State.

The odd zigzag in the North Carolina-South Carolina state line, just south of Charlotte, was created in 1772, when boundary commissioners altered the border to avoid splitting the Catawba Indians between the two British colonies.

Charlotte, North Carolina, was the gold-mining capitol of the United States from 1788 until 1848, when gold was discovered in California.

✳

The famous pirate Blackbeard's reign of terror ended off the coast of North Carolina in 1718. Lieutenant Robert Maynard, his vanquisher, sailed home with Blackbeard's head dangling from his ship.

✳

Sequoyah, a North Carolina Cherokee warrior, silversmith and painter, designed an alphabet for his language in 1821. Within two years most of his people could read and write. The alphabet contained 86 letters and combined characters from English, Hebrew, and Greek.

✳

Virginia extends 95 miles farther west than *West* Virginia.

✳

The Virginia colony adopted the pineapple as its the symbol for hospitality. The pineapple is still used as such, found over doorways, on furniture and as centerpieces.

✳

75 percent of West Virginia is covered in forest.

✳

Ted Turner (1938–) founded the country's first 24-hour news channel in Atlanta in 1980. It's called Cable News Network— or CNN.

"FOUR LITTLE GIRLS WERE KILLED..."

CHARLES B. MORGAN, JR.
BIRMINGHAM, ALABAMA, SEPTEMBER 16, 1963

The violence over segregation in Birmingham had reached a fever pitch when, on September 15, 1963, four African-American girls attending church were killed by a bomb. The next day, local white lawyer Charles B. Morgan addressed Birmingham's Young Businessman's Club.

FOUR LITTLE GIRLS were killed in Birmingham yesterday.

A mad, remorseful worried community asks, "Who did it? Who threw that bomb? Was it a Negro or a white?" The answer should be, "We all did it." Every last one of us is condemned for that crime and the bombing before it and a decade ago. We all did it.

A short time later, white policemen kill a Negro and wound another. A few hours later, two young men on a motorbike shoot and kill a Negro child. Fires break out, and, in Montgomery, white youths assault Negroes.

And all across Alabama, an angry, guilty people cry out their mocking shouts of indignity and say they wonder "Why?" "Who?" Everyone then "deplores" the "dastardly" act.

But you know the "who" of "Who did it" is really rather simple. The "who" is every little individual who talks about the "niggers" and spreads

the seeds of his hate to his neighbor and his son. The jokester, the crude oaf whose racial jokes rock the party with laughter.

The "who" is every governor who ever shouted for lawlessness and became a law violator.

It is every senator and every representative who in the halls of Congress stands and with mock humility tells the world that things back home aren't really like they are.

It is courts that move ever so slowly, and newspapers that timorously defend the law.

It is all the Christians and all their ministers who spoke too late in anguished cries against violence. It is the coward in each of us who clucks admonitions.

We have 10 years of lawless preachments, 10 years of criticism of law, of courts, of our fellow man, a decade of telling school children the opposite of what the civics books say.

We are a mass of intolerance and bigotry and stand indicted before our young. We are cursed by the failure of each of us to accept responsibility, by our defense of an already dead institution....

Birmingham is the only city in America where the police chief and the sheriff in the school crisis had to call our local ministers together to tell them to do their duty. The ministers of

Birmingham who have done so little for Christianity call for prayer at high noon in a city of lawlessness, and in the same breath, speak of our city's "image."...

Those four little Negro girls were human beings. They have their 14 years in a leaderless city; a city where no one accepts responsibility; where everybody wants to blame somebody else. A city with a reward fund which grew like Topsy as a sort of sacrificial offering, a balm for the conscience of the "good people."...

And, who is really guilty? Each of us. Each citizen who has not consciously attempted to bring about peaceful compliance with the decisions of the Supreme Court of the United States, every citizen and every school board member and schoolteacher and principal and businessman and judge and lawyer who has corrupted the minds of our youth; every person in this community who has in any way contributed during the past several years to the popularity of hatred, is at least as guilty, or more so, than the demented fool who threw that bomb.

What's it like living in Birmingham? No one ever really has known and no one will until this city becomes part of the United States.

Birmingham is not a dying city; it is dead.

BISCUITS & GRAVY

Today's basic biscuit is much easier on the jaw than the original "hardtack" biscuits served as Civil War rations. Called "tooth dullers" by the soldiers, they were served with a rich dipping gravy whenever possible.

Biscuits

½ cup lukewarm water

1 teaspoon active dry yeast

2 tablespoons sugar

2 ½ cups unbleached all-purpose flour

1 teaspoon baking powder

1 teaspoon salt

¼ cup vegetable shortening

4 tablespoons butter, chilled

¾ cup milk or buttermilk

1. In a small mixing bowl, whisk together the warm water, yeast and sugar. Set the mixture aside for 30 minutes. In a medium bowl, whisk together the flour, baking powder and salt. Cut in the shortening and butter, and mix until rough and crumbly.

2. Pour the milk or buttermilk into the yeast mixture, and add this to the dry ingredients. Fold together gently until the mixture leaves the sides of the bowl and becomes cohesive.

3. Turn the dough out onto a lightly floured work surface. Knead gently six times and form a ball. Pat it out until the dough is about ½″ thick. Use a glass to cut the dough into as many biscuits as you can. Gather the scraps gently and do it again.

4. Put the biscuits on a lightly greased or parchment-lined cookie sheet. Cover with a damp towel and let rise in a warm place for approximately 1 hour.

5. Preheat oven to 400° F.

6. Bake biscuits for 10–12 minutes.

Serves 6 to 8.

Gravy

1 pound pork
breakfast sausage,
bulk style,
chopped up

2 tablespoons flour

1 cup milk

salt and pepper
to taste

1. Fry the sausage until it is brown,
   breaking it up as you cook it.

2. Separate the cooked sausage from the drippings.
   Set the sausage aside.

3. Heat the drippings over a medium flame and slowly
   whisk in as much flour as there are drippings.
   Whisk and let bubble for 2–3 minutes.
   If the gravy is dry at this point, add some butter.

4. Add the milk, stirring vigorously, and bring it to a
   low boil. Simmer until it thickens (about 5 minutes).
   If it is too thick, add more milk. Add the sausage
   bits, and salt and pepper to taste.

   Pour over the warm biscuits or
   serve the gravy on the side.

The Southwest

Though Flagstaff, Arizona's Lowell Observatory was founded primarily to explore the possibility of life on Mars, it's better known for the discovery of the planet Pluto, in 1930.

Georgia O'Keefe's (1887–1986) paintings of stark skulls and vibrant desert vistas near her beloved New Mexico home immortalized the light and landscapes of the Southwest.

Each year Las Vegas is visited by 30 million people, who lose about $8 billion gambling, and spend another $8 billion on the state's tourism industry.

Las Vegas's chapels perform 110,000 marriages annually— about 300 a day.

Construction of the Hoover Dam, on the Colorado River, required more than 5 million barrels of cement.

The first atomic bomb was detonated in Alamogordo, New Mexico, on July 16, 1945.

Santa Fe, New Mexico was established by the Spaniards in 1610.

On April 18, 1934, America's first laundromat opened in Fort Worth, Texas.

Bracken Cave in Texas is home to the largest bat maternity colony in the world. Its 20 million Mexican free-tailed bats can consume up to 500,000 pounds of insects on a single summer night.

Covering 1300 square miles, Texas' King Ranch, founded in 1853, is bigger than the state of Rhode Island.

In 1977 the Texas State Legislature proclaimed chili the state's official dish.

"Juneteenth" is a real holiday. On June 19th, 1865, Texas slaves were freed under General Order #3. Today that's still celebrated in Texas, Louisiana, Arkansas and Oklahoma.

Considered the deadliest natural disaster in U.S. history, the 1900 hurricane that hit Galveston, Texas killed more than 6,000 people. The toll was greater than those of the Great Chicago Fire, the Johnstown, PA Flood and the San Francisco Earthquake and Fire—combined.

Dr. Pepper, America's first soft drink, was created in 1885 in Waco, Texas by Charles Alderton, who named it after his first boss.

Texas is the only state to allow absentee voting from anywhere in the universe. The first person to take advantage of that was astronaut David Wolf— whose ballot came from the space station Mir, in 1997.

THE YELLOW ROSE OF TEXAS

ANONYMOUS, 1858

There's a yellow rose in Texas that I am going to see,
No other soldier knows her, no soldier only me;
She cried so when I left her, it like to broke my heart,
And if I ever find her we never more will part.

Chorus
She's the sweetest little flower this soldier ever knew,
Her eyes are bright as diamonds, they sparkle like the dew,
You may talk about your Dearest May, and sing of Rosa Lee,
But the yellow rose of Texas beats the belles of Tennessee.

Where the Rio Grande is flowing, and the starry skies are bright,
She walks along the river in the quiet summer night;
She thinks if I remember when we parted long ago,
I promised to come back again, and not to leave her so.

Chorus
Oh, now I'm going to find her, for my heart is full of woe,
And we'll sing the song together, that we sung so long ago;
We'll play the banjo gaily, and we'll sing the songs of yore,
And the yellow rose of Texas shall be mine forevermore.